THE ULTIMATE BEGINNER'S GUIDE TO CONTAINER GARDENING

SMALL SPACE GARDENING MADE EASY—GROW YOUR OWN VEGETABLES, HERBS, AND FLOWERS EVEN IF YOU HAVE NO EXPERIENCE!

AVERY SAGE

VIBRANT CIRCLE BOOKS LLC

CONTENTS

Introduction   vii

1. GETTING STARTED WITH CONTAINER
   GARDENING   1
   Understanding Container Gardening: More Than Just
   a Garden in a Pot   1
   Choosing the Right Containers: Materials, Shapes,
   and Sizes   3
   Creating the Perfect Soil Mix for Containers   5
   Essential Tools for the Container Gardener   7
   Planning Your Garden Layout: Maximizing Small
   Spaces   10
   Interactive Layout Exercise   12
   Setting Realistic Expectations: What to Grow and
   How Much   13

2. SELECTING AND CARING FOR PLANTS   17
   Best Vegetables for Container Gardening: A
   Beginner's Guide   17
   Reflection Exercise: Your Ideal Vegetable Garden   20
   Herbs That Thrive in Containers and Small Spaces   21
   Flowering Plants for Year-Round Color and Interest   23
   Companion Planting in Containers: Plants That Grow
   Well Together   25
   Seasonal Planting: Timing Your Planting for Optimal
   Growth   27
   Plant Care Basics: Pruning, Deadheading, and
   Beyond   29

3. WATERING AND FERTILIZING ESSENTIALS   33
   Mastering the Art of Watering: Techniques for Busy
   Schedules   33
   Self-Watering Containers: A Time-Saving Solution   36
   Choosing the Right Fertilizer: Organic vs. Synthetic   38
   Feeding Your Plants: Nutrient Needs at Different
   Growth Stages   40

Reflection Section: Tracking Plant Health   41

Water Conservation Strategies for Eco-Conscious Gardeners   42

Troubleshooting Watering Issues: Overwatering and Underwatering   44

4. DESIGNING YOUR CONTAINER GARDEN   47

Vertical Gardening: Utilizing Height in Small Spaces   47

Interactive Element: Vertical Garden Planning Exercise   50

Creating Eye-Catching Arrangements: Color, Texture, and Form   50

DIY Container Projects: Upcycling and Creative Solutions   52

Designing with Succulents: Low-Maintenance Beauty   54

Creating a Pollinator-Friendly Garden in Containers   56

Reflection Section: Pollinator Observation Journal   58

Integrating Edibles and Ornamentals for a Functional Garden   59

Reflection Exercise: Mixed Garden Planning   61

Make a Difference with Your Review   63

5. DEALING WITH PESTS AND DISEASES   65

Identifying Common Pests in Container Gardens   65

Natural Pest Control: Eco-Friendly Solutions That Work   68

Preventing and Treating Fungal Diseases   70

Reflection Section: Your Fungal Battle Plan   72

Beneficial Insects: Nature's Pest Control   72

Crafting an Enticing Environment   73

Concerns and Balances   74

Embracing the Unseen Guardians   74

DIY Remedies for Pests: Recipes and Techniques   75

Creating a Healthy Ecosystem: Promoting Plant Resilience   77

6. ADAPTING TO CLIMATE CHALLENGES   81

Understanding Your Climate: Microclimates and Plant Hardiness   81

Interactive Element: Climate Mapping Exercise   83

Protecting Your Plants from Extreme Weather: Heat and Frost   83

Adapting to Seasonal Changes: Tips for Year-Round Gardening 86

Insightful Approaches to Seasonal Planning 87

Container Gardening in Arid Climates: Xeriscaping and More 88

Coping with Humidity: Plant Choices and Care Strategies 91

Winterizing Your Container Garden: Preparing for Cold Months 93

7. SUSTAINABLE AND ECO-FRIENDLY PRACTICES 97

Composting for Container Gardeners: Creating Your Own Fertilizer 97

Upcycling Containers: Creative and Sustainable Solutions 100

Water-Wise Gardening: Reducing Your Environmental Impact 102

Organic Gardening Practices: Safe and Natural Techniques 104

Building a Sustainable Container Garden: Long-Term Tips 107

Supporting Local Wildlife: Creating Habitats in Small Spaces 109

8. TROUBLESHOOTING AND SUCCESS STORIES 113

Common Container Gardening Mistakes and How to Avoid Them 113

Interactive Exercise: Planning Your Perfect Container Garden 114

Diagnosing Plant Problems: Symptoms and Solutions 115

Container Garden Troubleshooting Checklist 117

Testing & Monitoring Tips 119

Success Stories: Inspiring Journeys from Beginner to Pro 119

Learning from Failures: Turning Setbacks into Growth Opportunities 121

Community Connections: Joining the Container Gardening Movement 124

Planning for the Future: Expanding Your Gardening Horizons 126

Keep the Garden Growing   129
Conclusion   131
References   133

INTRODUCTION

A few years ago, I met a neighbor named Sarah. She lived in a tiny apartment with only a small balcony. Sarah had never gardened before but was determined to bring some greenery into her life. Armed with a few pots, some soil, and a handful of seeds, she transformed her little outdoor space into a vibrant container garden. Her tomatoes flourished, her herbs thrived, and colorful flowers brightened her mornings. Watching her joy, I realized how powerful container gardening could be for anyone with limited space.

Container gardening is more than a trend; it's a growing movement. In cities worldwide, people are turning their balconies and windowsills into small, productive gardens. According to recent studies, urban gardening has increased by over 30% in the past decade. Many people want fresh produce but lack the yard space to grow it. Container gardening offers a solution, allowing you to cultivate your own food and enjoy nature, even in compact spaces.

The purpose of this book is simple. I aim to provide step-by-step guidance for beginners. Whether you want to grow vegetables, herbs, or flowers, I'll show you how. You don't need to be an expert or have a large garden to succeed. With practical, easy-to-follow advice, you'll be able to nurture your own container garden.

Container gardening offers many benefits. It's flexible and space-efficient. You can move your containers to catch the sun or bring them inside when it's cold. You have control over the growing conditions, which means healthier plants. Plus, there's nothing quite like picking fresh produce from your own garden or enjoying the scent of blooming flowers.

I understand the concerns many beginners have. You might worry about not having enough experience or space. Rest assured, this book addresses these challenges. I'll provide practical solutions to help you get started and succeed. You'll learn about choosing the right containers, caring for your plants, and using eco-friendly practices. We'll cover watering techniques, soil selection, and plant care. By the end, you'll have the knowledge and confidence to create your own garden.

Container gardening is not just a hobby; it's a journey of growth and experimentation. Embrace the process. There will be successes and failures, and both are valuable. Each step you take is a chance to learn and improve. Enjoy the journey and watch your efforts blossom.

I invite you to join me on this adventure. Let's transform your space into a thriving container garden. Whether you have a balcony, patio, or just a sunny windowsill, you can cultivate your own green space. Together, we'll explore the joys of gardening and discover the transformative power it holds. Welcome to the start of your container gardening journey.

CHAPTER 1
GETTING STARTED WITH CONTAINER GARDENING

UNDERSTANDING CONTAINER GARDENING: MORE THAN JUST A GARDEN IN A POT

Container gardening is not just about sticking plants in pots; it's a versatile method that adapts to your lifestyle. At its core, it involves growing plants in containers rather than directly in the ground. This technique allows you to cultivate a variety of plants, from leafy greens to bright blooms, without needing a sprawling yard. The beauty of container gardening lies in its flexibility, making it perfect for urban dwellers with limited space.

One of the primary benefits of container gardening is mobility. You can move your plants to catch the sun or bring them indoors when the weather turns nasty. This versatility means you can grow plants in places you might not have considered, like windowsills or rooftops. It's also incredibly accessible. You don't need a lot of tools or expertise to get started—just some containers, soil, and seeds. In urban environments, container gardening offers a solution to space constraints, letting you enjoy fresh produce and beautiful plants right at home.

However, like any endeavor, it comes with its challenges. Space-saving is a significant advantage since you can grow vertically or stack pots, but it also means you're working with limited soil volume. This can affect nutrient retention and water supply. Containers dry out faster than ground soil, so keeping your plants hydrated becomes crucial. But don't worry—these challenges are easily managed with the right strategies.

The creativity that container gardening allows is unmatched. You can arrange containers in various ways to suit your aesthetic preferences and functional needs. Consider mixing edibles like herbs and vegetables with ornamentals for a visually stunning and practical garden. The possibilities are endless—hanging baskets, tiered setups, or even repurposed items like teapots or boots can become unique planters. Your garden becomes an extension of your personality, allowing for endless experimentation.

Embracing sustainability is also key in container gardening. Upcycling materials for containers not only gives them a second life but also adds character to your garden. Look around your home for items that could be transformed into pots—a chipped mug or an old crate can work wonders. Sustainable practices extend to soil and fertilizer choices as well. Opt for organic options that nourish your plants while being kind to the environment.

Container gardening is both an art and a science, offering a rewarding experience for those willing to dive into its world. You'll find that each plant you nurture teaches you something new about growth and resilience. As you experiment and learn, remember that mistakes are part of the process. They lead to discoveries and solutions that improve your gardening skills.

The benefits you reap from container gardening go beyond the fresh herbs or bright flowers you grow. It's about creating a slice of nature that brings joy and tranquility to your life, no matter where you live. This chapter is just the beginning of your journey into this green adventure, where every pot holds the potential for something beautiful.

As we continue, we'll explore the practical aspects of setting up your container garden—choosing the right containers and soil, essential tools, and planning your layout. Each step will build your confidence and skills, turning your space into a thriving garden filled with life and color.

So let's get started on this exciting path, transforming your space one pot at a time into an oasis of beauty and growth.

CHOOSING THE RIGHT CONTAINERS: MATERIALS, SHAPES, AND SIZES

When it comes to container gardening, selecting the right containers is a pivotal decision that sets the foundation for your plant's health and growth. Let's start with materials. Terracotta pots are classic choices, known for their earthy aesthetic and breathability. They allow air and moisture to flow through the sides, which can help prevent root rot. However, they tend to be heavy and can crack in cold weather. Plastic containers, on the other hand, are lightweight and affordable. They retain moisture well, making them suitable for plants that require consistent hydration. But, they might not offer the same breathability as terracotta. Metal containers bring a modern touch to your garden with their sleek appearance, yet they can heat up quickly in direct sunlight, potentially harming sensitive roots. Understanding these nuances helps you decide what's best for your garden's needs.

Considering size and shape is just as crucial. The container's size dictates how much room your plant's roots have to grow. A container that is too small can stunt growth, while one that is too large can lead to waterlogging if the soil retains too much moisture. When choosing a container, ensure it has adequate drainage holes. Good drainage prevents water from sitting at the bottom, which can drown roots. For larger plants or those with extensive root systems, like tomatoes or peppers, opt for deeper pots. Shallow containers work well for herbs or succulents that don't require much root space. The shape of the container not only affects aesthetics but also how you arrange your plants. Tall, narrow pots can create height and drama, while wide, shallow ones can accommodate a lush arrangement of ground cover plants.

Beyond practicality, consider the aesthetic and functional aspects of your containers. Your garden should reflect your personal style and fit seamlessly into your living space. If your home leans towards a minimalist design, sleek metal or simple ceramic pots might complement it best. For a rustic feel, terracotta or wooden containers add warmth and texture. Space efficiency is also key, especially in small areas. Vertical planters or stacking pots can maximize space by allowing you to grow upwards rather than outwards. These options not only save space but also create eye-catching displays.

Maintaining your containers ensures they remain in top condition season after season. Regular cleaning prevents disease spread and keeps them looking fresh. For terracotta and ceramic pots, scrub them with a mixture of water and vinegar to remove mineral deposits and algae. Plastic containers benefit from a simple soap and water wash, while metal pots may require a gentle wipe to prevent rusting. Proper storage extends a container's lifespan; during harsh weather, store them in a shed or garage to protect them from cracking due to freezing temperatures.

Container Selection Checklist

- **Choose Materials Wisely**: Consider the pros and cons of terracotta, plastic, and metal.
- **Assess Size and Shape**: Ensure adequate root space and drainage.
- **Blend Aesthetics with Functionality**: Match designs with home decor and maximize space.

- **Regular Maintenance**: Clean thoroughly and store properly to extend lifespan.

Selecting containers thoughtfully sets your garden up for success. It's not just about where you place your plants but how you support their journey from seedling to mature beauty. With these considerations in mind, you're better equipped to create a thriving container garden that mirrors your personal style and meets your plants' needs, turning every pot into a statement of growth and creativity in your space.

CREATING THE PERFECT SOIL MIX FOR CONTAINERS

Soil is the foundation of any garden, but in container gardening, it plays an even more critical role. Unlike garden beds, where soil can naturally replenish nutrients and moisture, containers are limited environments. This means that the soil you choose must be top-notch. It needs to retain enough nutrients to feed your plants while having excellent drainage and aeration. Poor-quality soil can lead to waterlogged roots or nutrient deficiencies, which spell trouble for your plants. Think of your container soil as a blank canvas—what you mix into it determines the masterpiece you'll create.

A well-rounded soil mix starts with the basics: peat moss, perlite, and vermiculite. Peat moss serves as the backbone by retaining moisture and providing a lightweight structure. Perlite, those little white particles you often see, improves aeration and drainage, essential for healthy root growth. Vermiculite adds another layer of water retention but also aids in nutrient retention, keeping your plants well-fed. These three components work in harmony to create a balanced environment within your containers.

Beyond these basics, organic additives like compost enrich the soil with essential nutrients. Compost is nature's way of recycling nutrients back into the soil, providing a slow-release fertilizer that benefits your plants over time. It adds microorganisms that break down organic matter, boosting soil health. Incorporating compost into your mix not only enhances nutrient content but also improves moisture retention and aeration. For those seeking an extra nutrient boost, a sprinkle of worm castings can work wonders, adding beneficial bacteria and nutrients.

Crafting your own soil mix is both satisfying and cost-effective. Start with a basic recipe: two parts peat moss, one part perlite, one part vermiculite, and a generous portion of compost. Adjust these ratios based on your plant's specific needs; for instance, more perlite for succulents that require excellent drainage or more compost for nutrient-hungry vegetables. Mix thoroughly in a large container or wheelbarrow, ensuring an even distribution of materials. This DIY approach allows you to tailor the mix to your plants, optimizing their growth conditions.

Testing and amending your soil is crucial for maintaining optimal plant health. Begin by assessing the pH level, which determines nutrient availability. Most plants prefer a slightly acidic to neutral pH, around 6 to 7. Simple pH testing kits are available at garden centers and provide quick results. If adjustments are necessary, adding lime can raise the pH, while sulfur can lower it. These amendments should be made gradually and with caution, as drastic changes can shock your plants.

Soil Testing Tips

- **Use a Reliable Kit**: Invest in a quality pH testing kit for accurate readings.
- **Test Regularly**: Check pH levels seasonally to adapt to changes.
- **Amend Gradually**: Adjust pH levels slowly over time to prevent plant stress.

Regularly refreshing your soil is another key component of container gardening success. Over time, soil can become compacted and depleted of nutrients. Every season or two, consider emptying containers and mixing in fresh compost or new soil mix to invigorate the growing medium. This practice ensures that your plants have a continuous supply of nutrients and an environment conducive to healthy root development.

While creating the perfect soil mix may seem daunting at first, it's easier than it appears. Focus on understanding the needs of your plants and adjusting accordingly. A thoughtful approach to soil preparation sets the stage for vibrant growth and flourishing gardens.

The beauty of container gardening lies in these small yet impactful choices that empower you to cultivate thriving plants. Your attention to detail in selecting and mixing soil reflects your commitment to nurturing life in every pot and planter you tend.

By prioritizing soil quality and understanding its nuances, you're not just planting seeds but cultivating an environment where they can thrive and reach their full potential.

ESSENTIAL TOOLS FOR THE CONTAINER GARDENER

Stepping into the world of container gardening, it's easy to get overwhelmed by the array of tools available. However, you don't need a shed full of gadgets to succeed. Start with the basics, and you'll find that the right tools can make your gardening experience both enjoyable and productive. Let's explore a few must-haves that every beginner should consider adding to their collection.

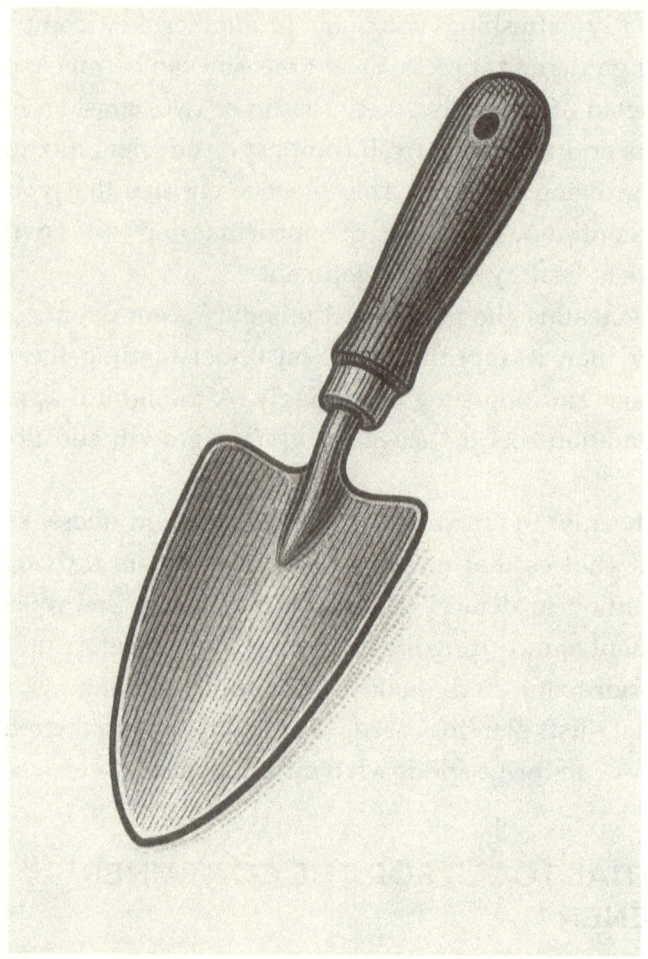

Typical trowel

First on our list is the trusty trowel. This small but mighty tool will become your best friend as you dig into various tasks. From planting to transplanting and even weeding, a trowel's pointed blade allows you to navigate tight spaces with ease. Look for one with a comfortable handle that fits snugly in your hand, reducing strain during extended use. To keep your trowel in top condition, rinse it after each use to remove soil and debris, then dry it thoroughly to prevent rust. Store it in a dry place, preferably hanging on a peg or tucked away in a tool caddy.

Next up is the watering can. While any container can technically be used for watering, choosing a can with a long spout gives you precise control over where the water goes. This feature is particularly useful for reaching deep into pots without drenching the leaves, which can lead to disease. Opt for a can that holds enough water for your needs but isn't so heavy when full that it becomes cumbersome to carry. After each use, empty any remaining water to prevent algae buildup and store it upside down to ensure it dries completely.

Pruners are another essential tool in your gardening arsenal. These sharp scissors help you trim and shape plants, encouraging healthy growth and preventing disease spread. When selecting pruners, choose a pair that feels balanced and comfortable in your hand. For maintenance, clean the blades with soapy water after use and apply a light coat of oil to keep them lubricated and rust-free. Regular sharpening ensures they're always ready for action.

While these three tools form the core of your gardening kit, there are a few extras that can enhance efficiency and ease your workload. Self-watering systems, for instance, are a game-changer for those who travel frequently or have busy schedules. These systems deliver consistent moisture directly to the plant's roots, reducing the risk of overwatering and keeping your plants happy even when you're away.

A portable gardening bench is another handy addition. It provides a comfortable spot to sit or kneel while working on your plants, and many models include storage compartments for your tools. This setup keeps everything you need within arm's reach and saves you from unnecessary trips back and forth.

For those looking to streamline their tasks further, consider investing in quality gloves to protect your hands from thorns and blisters. A soil scoop can make transferring potting mix into containers less messy, while plant labels help you keep track of what's growing where. Each tool you add should serve a purpose and make your gardening experience more enjoyable.

. . .

Tool Maintenance Tips

- **Clean Regularly**: Rinse soil off tools after use.
- **Dry Thoroughly**: Prevent rust by drying tools completely.
- **Store Properly**: Hang or place tools in a dry area to avoid moisture damage.

Remember, it's not about having every tool on the market but rather selecting those that suit your specific needs and enhance your gardening experience. Over time, as you become more comfortable with container gardening, you might find yourself drawn to specialty tools that cater to unique tasks or particular plant types. Embrace this process of discovery—each tool you add is another step towards creating the garden you've envisioned.

Container gardening is about making the most of what you have, both in terms of space and resources. With these essential tools by your side, you'll be well-equipped to tackle any gardening challenge that comes your way. Whether you're planting seeds or nurturing mature plants, these tools will support your efforts and help ensure success.

PLANNING YOUR GARDEN LAYOUT: MAXIMIZING SMALL SPACES

In the realm of container gardening, optimizing space is a thrilling challenge, akin to piecing together an intricate puzzle. Picture your small balcony or patio as a blank canvas, a space brimming with potential just waiting to be unlocked by your creativity and careful planning. Vertical gardening becomes your paintbrush, allowing you to add both layers and depth to your design landscape. With a handful of the right techniques, you can transform this limited area into a lush, tranquil green sanctuary. Consider using sturdy materials like reclaimed wood for shelves or rustic iron for hanging baskets to elevate your plants, crafting a tiered effect that draws the eye upward and creates a sense of expansiveness. Walls and railings naturally serve as invaluable allies; they provide robust support for climbing plants such as sweet peas or morning glories, which can cascade gracefully over the edges, adding not just texture but also an undeniable charm and vibrancy to your space.

The arrangement of your plants in this miniature Eden is crucial, not only for aesthetics but also for achieving full functionality. Think of your garden as a living mosaic, a canvas of ever-shifting patterns and hues. Start by thoughtfully coordinating colors to create visual harmony that pleases not only the eye but also the soul. Group plants with similar hues—deep purples with lush greens or sunny yellows with vibrant reds—or choose contrasting shades for a striking, unforgettable effect. Height also plays a significant role; wisely place taller plants like verdant tomatoes or radiant sunflowers towards the back or center, with their shorter counterparts, such as fragrant herbs, in front. This creates a meticulously layered look, ensuring each plant, with its innate beauty, gets its moment in the spotlight without overshadowing its neighbors. Consider the changing seasons in your layout. Plan so that as one plant fades into dormancy, another comes into vibrant bloom, sustaining a dynamic and ever-evolving landscape.

Sunlight, the lifeblood of any thriving garden, holds the power to make all the difference in your gardening endeavor. Positioning your plants to maximize sunlight involves a bit more than simply placing them in direct sunlight. Consider the natural orientation of your space. A south-facing window or balcony typically receives the most sunlight throughout the day, creating the perfect environment for sun-loving plants like fiery peppers or aromatic basil. Meanwhile, east or west-facing spaces may catch only partial sun, which accommodates shade-tolerant plants such as feathery ferns or crisp lettuce. Remember, even within small areas, intriguing microclimates exist. Observe and understand how light shifts and varies in different spots, perhaps due to shading from neighboring trees, buildings, or even architectural features of your structure.

Microclimates are truly fascinating phenomena; they offer distinct growing conditions that, when explored wisely, can be leveraged to your advantage. Perhaps you discover a nook that stays warmer during the brisk winter or cooler amid the scorching summer heat. Use these subtle nuances to your benefit when deciding the perfect placements for your containers. For instance, a spot near a brick wall might retain heat longer into the evening, nurturing warmth-loving plants to flourish. Conversely, areas that naturally catch soothing breezes can help cool down heat-sensitive species during the hottest months of the year, ensuring their comfort and survival.

INTERACTIVE LAYOUT EXERCISE

Let's dive into a hands-on approach. Grab a piece of paper and sketch your space to embark on this creative journey. Plot where sunlight falls at different times of day, marking areas that bask in morning light against those shaded in the afternoon. Identify any existing structures like walls or railings, noting them as potential assets in your plan. Visualize how you might incorporate vertical elements, or how you could use color and height to design your living masterpiece. This strategic exercise primes you to plan thoughtfully and efficiently before purchasing plants, optimizing not only your space but also your budget.

By embracing these detailed techniques, your small space can transform into a thriving garden replete with layers of interest, beauty, and personality, all tailored to your unique environment and creative vision. In no time, your small yet mighty garden will stand as a testament to your dedication, thriving in flawless harmony with its surroundings.

SETTING REALISTIC EXPECTATIONS: WHAT TO GROW AND HOW MUCH

Stepping into the world of container gardening can be both exhilarating and daunting. It's essential to set realistic goals that honor your space, time, and resources. Start small. Imagine you're dipping your toes into the water rather than diving headfirst. Herbs like basil, mint, and parsley are perfect for beginners. They're forgiving, grow quickly, and offer immediate satisfaction as you snip fresh leaves for your culinary creations. If you're inclined towards vegetables, consider starting with lettuce or radishes. These are quick to harvest and don't demand much space. A small success here and there boosts confidence and sets the stage for more ambitious projects. (We'll delve more into selecting plants in the next chapter.)

When you begin this venture, understanding plant growth cycles is crucial. Each plant has its own rhythm and timeline. For example, tomatoes may take a few months to mature, while radishes can be ready in just a few weeks. Knowing these timelines helps you plan your garden activities and manage expectations. Additionally, be aware of the expected yield per container. A single tomato plant might fill a large pot and yield several pounds of fruit throughout the season, whereas a basil plant in a smaller pot could provide fresh leaves for months with regular pruning. Understanding these cycles allows you to plan meals around your harvest.

As you gain experience, scaling your garden becomes a natural progression. It's like building a collection of favorite books—one addition at a time. You might start with a few pots on the windowsill, then expand to hanging baskets or larger containers as you grow more confident. Introduce new plants gradually, allowing yourself time to learn their specific needs. Maybe add a pot of cherry tomatoes or a container of vibrant marigolds to attract pollinators. Slowly, your garden transforms into a thriving ecosystem.

Rotational planting is an excellent strategy as you expand. This technique involves swapping out plants as they finish their growth cycle to make the most of your space. For instance, after harvesting spring lettuce, replace it with summer peppers or eggplants. This approach keeps your garden productive throughout the year, offering a variety of crops and flowers to enjoy each season.

Growth Timeline Reference

To help you plan better, here's a simple chart of growth timelines for common container plants:

- **Basil**: 4-6 weeks until first harvest
- **Tomatoes**: 60-80 days until first harvest
- **Radishes**: 3-4 weeks
- **Lettuce**: 4-6 weeks
- **Peppers**: 70-85 days

This list isn't exhaustive, but it gives you an idea of what to expect as you start planting.

Finally, remember that gardening is as much about the experience as it is about the results. Every plant teaches you something new, whether it's how to adjust watering schedules or how sunlight shifts throughout the year. Celebrate every sprout and bloom as milestones in your gardening adventure. Mistakes will happen—they're part of the learning process. Embrace them as opportunities for growth rather than setbacks.

As you nurture your plants, you'll find that your garden becomes an extension of yourself—a reflection of your care and creativity. Whether you're growing herbs for the kitchen or flowers for the sheer joy they bring, every effort contributes to cultivating beauty in your life.

With these insights and strategies at hand, you're ready to set realistic expectations and grow your garden with confidence and enthusiasm. Each step you take enriches not just your space but also your understanding and appreciation of nature's wonders.

CHAPTER 2
SELECTING AND CARING FOR PLANTS

BEST VEGETABLES FOR CONTAINER GARDENING: A BEGINNER'S GUIDE

Imagine waking up, stepping onto your small balcony, and picking fresh lettuce leaves for your lunchtime sandwich that day. This isn't just a reverie confined to dreams—it's something utterly tangible and achievable, even if you're stepping into the world of gardening without any prior experience. Container gardening unveils a realm of endless possibilities, especially when it comes to cultivating your very own vegetables. Let us embark on a journey to explore a selection of vegetables that are exceptionally easy to grow, making them perfect candidates for beginners like you. Leafy greens such as lettuce and spinach emerge as fantastic choices. They thrive admirably within the confines of a container and exhibit swift growth, gracing you with a continuous and plentiful supply of fresh, verdant leaves. These plants exhibit a remarkable resilience and adaptability; they don't demand much space, rendering them ideal for urban gardening settings where space is often a luxury. In addition to their minimalistic space needs, they're forgiving companions who won't hold a grudge if you happen to miss a watering or two.

Root vegetables, including radishes and carrots, have also proven their mettle in container settings. Radishes, with their rapid growth cycle, are tailor-made for the impatient gardener who eagerly anticipates visible progress. Carrots, while calling for deeper containers to accommodate their length, reward your patience with crunchy textures and a burst of sweet flavor. Opting for these particular vegetables is a wise starting point for embarking on your container gardening journey. The key to success lies in selecting compact, adaptable varieties that harmonize with limited spaces. When browsing seed catalogs or garden centers, keep an eye out for varieties labeled as "baby" or "dwarf," as they are expertly tailored for small spaces and will still yield a gratifying harvest.

Understanding the intricate space and light requirements of your chosen vegetables stands as a cornerstone of successful container gardening. Compact living spaces necessitate meticulous planning, urging you to select varieties that align with your spatial limitations. If you happen upon a sunny corner or spot on your patio, seize the opportunity by planting sun-loving vegetables like tomatoes or peppers that bask and grow luxuriously under ample sunlight. Conversely, if your area leans toward the shaded side, lean towards leafy greens that exhibit a remarkable tolerance for lower light levels and continue to flourish.

Growing vegetables in containers is a straightforward process that begins with selecting the appropriate container size. This initial step is crucial as it ensures your seeds have the necessary space and depth to thrive. For beginners, understanding that different vegetables have varying requirements is key. For instance, leafy greens such as lettuce and spinach are particularly adaptable and can be directly sown into pots without much fuss. These vegetables don't require deep soil to flourish, making them ideal choices for your first foray into container gardening. When planting radishes, it's important to space them a few inches apart. This spacing allows each radish enough room to grow both above and below the soil. Crowded plants often fail to develop properly, leading to a disappointing harvest. Therefore, paying attention to the spacing recommendations for each type of vegetable you plant can significantly impact your gardening success. Carrots, on the other hand, demand pots that are deeper than what most other vegetables require. This is because carrots need to extend their roots deep into the soil as they grow. Choosing a container that is too shallow will stunt their growth and result in undersized carrots. It's advisable to opt for pots that are at least 12 inches deep for these root vegetables, ensuring they have ample space to reach their full potential. Watering your container garden consistently is another critical aspect of growing vegetables. Uneven watering can lead to various problems, including bolting, where plants grow quickly but produce fewer leaves and flowers, or the development of bitter-tasting greens. To avoid these issues, establish a regular watering schedule. Vegetables in containers often require more frequent watering than those in the ground, as soil in pots can dry out quickly, especially in warm weather. Monitor the soil moisture level closely, and adjust your watering routine as needed to keep the soil evenly moist, not waterlogged or bone dry. By following these guidelines, you'll set the stage for a productive and enjoyable container gardening experience.

As you delve into container gardening, prepare for potential hurdles like pests or bolting. Aphids may become unwelcome tenants on your plants, but there's no need for alarm—natural remedies stand at the ready to address these nuisances. Employing neem oil or concocting a homemade soap spray stands as an effective measure to keep them at bay, steering clear of harsh chemicals and aligning with sustainable gardening practices. Bolting, mentioned in the last paragraph, also tends to occur in warmer weather. To counteract this, consider scheduling the planting of cool-season crops either early in spring or later in the fall when milder temperatures prevail. (We'll delve into common pests and diseases more in Chapter 5.)

Closeup of an aphid

REFLECTION EXERCISE: YOUR IDEAL VEGETABLE GARDEN

Pause for a moment to conjure an image of your ideal vegetable container garden. Consider what delights you envision cultivating, and meticulously jot down the vegetables that ignite your excitement the most. Take into account their space and light prerequisites for an informed and strategic plan. Reflect on the harmony between these chosen vegetables and the space available to you, contemplating any necessary adjustments to ensure their optimal growth.

By embarking with these beginner-friendly vegetables, you are meticulously laying the foundation for a flourishing venture into container gardening. The unparalleled joy of harvesting produce nurtured by your own hands and care is one of life's simple pleasures. With a sprinkle of dedication, a dash of attention, and an abundance of enthusiasm, you'll soon revel in the magnificent fruits (and vegetables) of your labor, savoring a vibrant, homegrown bounty.

HERBS THAT THRIVE IN CONTAINERS AND SMALL SPACES

Imagine a sunny afternoon, and you're in your kitchen preparing a meal. You reach over to your windowsill and pluck a few fresh basil leaves, their aroma instantly filling the air. This is the charm of growing herbs in containers, making them accessible and practical for any meal. Herbs like basil, mint, and parsley are not only easy to grow but also become integral to your culinary repertoire. Basil, with its lush, aromatic leaves, thrives in warm conditions and adds a sweet, peppery flavor to dishes. Mint spreads quickly, offering a refreshing taste perfect for teas or garnishes. Parsley, appreciated for its versatility, complements a wide range of recipes. These herbs are beginner-friendly, forgiving of slight neglect, and bounce back with a bit of care.

For those seeking more lasting companions, consider perennial herbs like thyme and rosemary. These resilient plants add depth to your garden with their woody stems and fragrant leaves. Thyme's small, hardy leaves pack a punch of flavor, while rosemary's needle-like foliage releases a rich aroma, perfect for roasts or stews. Both herbs thrive in well-drained soil and sunny spots, rewarding you with year-round harvests without demanding constant attention.

Planting and caring for herbs require understanding their unique needs. Good drainage is paramount; ensure your containers have holes to prevent waterlogging. Most herbs prefer full sun but can tolerate partial shade. The key to thriving herbs lies in regular harvesting. Snipping leaves not only provides you with fresh ingredients but also encourages new growth, keeping plants bushy and productive. Be mindful of overwatering—herbs prefer slightly dry conditions between watering sessions.

The choice between indoor and outdoor growing depends on your space and preferences. Indoor herb gardens thrive on sunny windowsills, offering convenience and quick access while cooking. However, they may need supplemental lighting during darker months. Outdoor options like balconies or patios provide more room for expansive growth, allowing herbs to bask in natural sunlight and fresh air. Outdoor settings also offer the opportunity to companion plant with other container vegetables or flowers.

Propagation is a rewarding way to expand your herb collection without breaking the bank. Mint and basil are particularly easy to propagate using cuttings. For mint, select a healthy stem around 4 inches long, remove the lower leaves, and place it in water until roots form. Once roots are visible, transfer it to a pot with well-draining soil. Basil follows a similar process; simply snip a stem below a leaf node, and watch as roots develop in water. These techniques not only extend your garden but also offer endless opportunities for sharing plants with friends or experimenting with new varieties.

Growing herbs in containers is a delightful endeavor that brings fresh flavors and vibrant scents to your home. It's about more than just planting seeds; it's creating a living pantry that enhances your meals and adds beauty to your space. Whether you're an avid cook or simply enjoy the occasional fresh garnish, container gardening allows you to cultivate an array of herbs tailored to your tastes and lifestyle.

FLOWERING PLANTS FOR YEAR-ROUND COLOR AND INTEREST

Marigolds, with their fiery orange and yellow petals, thrive in containers and are ideal for beginners. They're hardy, resist pests, and bloom throughout the season. Petunias add a touch of elegance with their continuous blooms, painting your garden in shades of pink, purple, and white. These flowers don't just look pretty; they bring your space to life, inviting pollinators like bees and butterflies.

To keep your garden lively all year, consider planting with the seasons in mind. Cool-season flowers like pansies and violas flourish in the fall and winter. They withstand cooler temperatures and add much-needed color during the dreary months. As spring warms up, switch to warm-season blooms like zinnias and cosmos. These plants bask in the sunlight and thrive in the heat, ensuring your garden stays colorful through summer. By rotating flowers with the seasons, you maintain a dynamic garden that never loses its charm.

Arranging flowers for visual impact is an art form. Mixing colors and textures can transform your space into a living master-piece. Combine bold hues with softer pastels for a striking contrast. Consider the texture of leaves and petals—pairing smooth with jagged edges creates an intriguing display. Trailing plants like sweet potato vine or ivy add height and depth, cascading over the edges of containers and drawing the eye. Layering plants by height ensures each one gets its moment to shine, creating a balanced and harmonious arrangement.

Flowering plants come with their own set of challenges, but with a little know-how, you can tackle them head-on. Deadheading, or removing spent blooms, encourages continuous flowering. This simple task redirects energy from seed production back into growth, keeping your plants vibrant. Pests like aphids might make an appearance, but don't fret. Natural solutions like neem oil or insecticidal soap keep them under control without harming beneficial insects. Regularly inspect your plants for signs of trouble—a quick intervention can prevent bigger issues down the line.

Whether you're new to gardening or a seasoned pro, flowering plants offer endless opportunities to experiment and express yourself. They bring joy not just through their blooms but also through the process of nurturing them to life. As you explore different varieties and arrangements, remember that gardening is as much about the journey as it is about the destination. Each season brings new challenges and rewards, keeping your passion for gardening alive.

Creating a garden filled with year-round color isn't just about choosing the right plants; it's about understanding how they interact with each other and their environment. Light, water, and soil all play critical roles in plant health. Pay attention to these elements, adjusting as needed to suit each plant's preferences. For instance, marigolds thrive in full sun while pansies prefer partial shade. Matching plants to their ideal conditions ensures they put on their best show.

Your garden reflects your personality—a canvas where you can play with colors, textures, and forms. Don't be afraid to experiment with unconventional combinations or try new plants each season. The beauty of container gardening lies in its flexibility; you can rearrange plants or swap them out as your tastes change. This adaptability keeps your garden fresh and exciting, a true reflection of your evolving style.

As you explore the world of flowering plants, you'll find that each one has its own story to tell. From towering sunflowers to delicate violas, they bring diverse colors and shapes to your garden. Embrace their uniqueness, learning from their successes and setbacks alike. With patience and care, you'll cultivate not just a garden but a living testament to your creativity and passion for nature's beauty.

COMPANION PLANTING IN CONTAINERS: PLANTS THAT GROW WELL TOGETHER

Companion planting is an ancient gardening practice that can transform your container garden into a thriving ecosystem. Imagine your plants as friendly neighbors who help each other grow better and stay healthy. By placing them together, you can naturally repel pests and enhance flavor, all while maximizing space. Picture tomatoes and basil growing side by side. The basil has a knack for deterring pesky insects that often target tomatoes. In return, the tomatoes provide a bit of shade, helping basil thrive. Plus, the flavor combination is unbeatable when it comes to making sauces or salads.

Let's consider carrots and onions. This duo works like a charm. Onions emit a scent that can confuse and deter carrot root flies, keeping your carrots safe from pests. These two not only protect each other but also make efficient use of space since they grow at different levels—onions above ground and carrots below. This is what companion planting is all about: creating harmonious partnerships that benefit everyone involved.

When planning your garden, it's vital to think about the available space and how plants interact underground. Roots need room to spread and access nutrients without competing aggressively. Layering plants based on root depth can help manage this effectively. For instance, shallow-rooted herbs can share a pot with deep-rooted vegetables because they won't compete for the same resources. Always ensure each plant has enough room for its roots to expand comfortably.

Experimentation is the spice of gardening. Don't hesitate to try new combinations and see what works best in your containers.

Keep a gardening journal to track what you plant together, how they perform, and any changes you notice. Write down everything from the date of planting to any pests you spot. Over time, you'll gather a wealth of knowledge about what specific pairings thrive in your unique conditions.

This approach not only makes gardening more engaging but also helps you learn from both successes and mishaps. You might find that some plants unexpectedly flourish together, while others don't get along as well as anticipated. The beauty of container gardening is its flexibility—if something doesn't work, it's easy to rearrange plants or try different groups without much hassle.

Beyond the practical benefits, companion planting adds an element of creativity to your garden design. Mix different colors and textures to create visually stunning displays. Let trailing plants like nasturtiums spill over the edges of pots while tall sunflowers stand proudly behind them. This layering not only maximizes space but also enhances the aesthetic appeal of your garden.

As you delve deeper into companion planting, you'll discover that certain combinations offer surprising perks. For instance, marigolds planted near cucumbers can deter nematodes and attract pollinators, boosting overall plant health and yield. Similarly, lettuce planted alongside chives benefits from the chives' natural pest-repellent properties while enjoying the shade provided by taller plants.

One thing to remember is that not all plant pairings are beneficial. Some combinations can lead to increased competition for resources or attract pests rather than deter them. Avoid pairing dill with carrots, as they compete for nutrients and may attract undesirable insects.

The key to successful companion planting is understanding the needs and behaviors of each plant species. Invest time in observing how they interact with one another and their environment. Pay attention to factors like sunlight exposure, watering schedules, and soil conditions.

Experimenting with companion planting not only enhances your garden's productivity but also deepens your understanding of plant interactions and ecosystems. As you continue exploring different combinations, you'll develop a keen sense of what works best in your specific environment, allowing you to create a thriving container garden that's both beautiful and productive.

SEASONAL PLANTING: TIMING YOUR PLANTING FOR OPTIMAL GROWTH

Timing is everything in gardening. Just like planning a vacation or scheduling your favorite show, knowing when to plant can make or break your success. Seasonal planting is about aligning your gardening efforts with nature's rhythms. It's about understanding frost dates and growing seasons, those pivotal moments that dictate when seedlings can safely venture outside. Every region has its own climate quirks, and getting familiar with yours is like learning the secret handshake to successful gardening.

Start by marking frost dates on your calendar. The last frost date is typically when it's safe to plant tender seedlings outdoors, while the first frost date signals the end of the growing season. These dates vary based on your location, so a little research goes a long way. Online tools and gardening apps make it super easy to find this information, often providing regional planting guides tailored to your area. Armed with this knowledge, you can plan your planting calendar like a seasoned pro.

Creating a planting schedule doesn't have to be as complicated as it sounds. Begin by jotting down what you want to grow and when it should be planted. Consider the time each plant needs to mature and work backward from the first frost date to determine the best planting time. This approach allows for rotational planting, where you stagger plantings of short-season crops like radishes or lettuce. As one batch finishes, sow another, ensuring a continuous harvest. This technique maximizes yield and keeps your garden productive throughout the year.

Succession planting is another gem in the gardener's toolkit. It's all about keeping your garden buzzing with activity by planting new crops as others fade out. Imagine harvesting peas in early summer, then using the same space for bush beans or late-season greens. By staggering planting times, you create a dynamic garden that provides fresh produce over an extended period. This approach not only enhances productivity but also allows for experimenting with different crops and varieties.

Of course, nature has a mind of its own, and seasonal changes can throw a wrench in even the best-laid plans. Unexpected weather shifts are part and parcel of gardening, but with a little preparation, you can navigate these challenges with ease. Protecting plants from sudden cold snaps or heat waves involves creative solutions like row covers or shade cloths. These simple tools act as barriers against extreme conditions, providing a buffer that keeps plants happy and healthy.

Transitioning plants between seasons requires thoughtful attention. As temperatures drop in autumn, consider moving tender perennials into more sheltered spots or indoors if possible. Adjust watering schedules and reduce feeding as growth slows during cooler months. Preparing for seasonal transitions ensures plants remain robust and resilient, ready to flourish when conditions improve.

Gardening is a dance with nature, where timing and adaptability are your best allies. By tuning into seasonal rhythms and planning accordingly, you set the stage for a thriving garden that mirrors nature's cycles. Whether it's synchronizing with frost dates or embracing succession planting, these strategies empower you to make informed decisions that elevate your gardening game.

As you continue exploring seasonal planting, remember that each year brings new opportunities to refine your approach. Keep track of what works well and where improvements can be made.

This ongoing process of learning and adapting enriches your understanding of plant behavior and enhances your connection to the natural world.

In this gardening dance, every plant has its season—embracing this idea helps you cultivate a garden that's not only productive but also deeply rewarding.

PLANT CARE BASICS: PRUNING, DEADHEADING, AND BEYOND

Imagine your garden as a living tapestry, where each plant plays a vital role. Just like any masterpiece, it requires regular upkeep to maintain its vibrancy. Pruning and deadheading are two key techniques that help keep your plants looking their best. Pruning is akin to giving your plant a haircut—it shapes and maintains its health by removing dead or overgrown branches. This not only enhances airflow but also reduces the risk of disease. For most plants, you'll want to prune in early spring before new growth begins, using sharp pruners or scissors to make clean cuts just above a leaf node or bud.

Deadheading, on the other hand, focuses on flowers. It involves snipping off spent blooms to encourage new ones. This simple practice redirects the plant's energy from seed production back into flowering, prolonging the bloom period. Using a pair of small scissors or your fingers, pinch off the faded flowers just below the base. Deadheading can be done throughout the growing season, and it's a great way to keep your garden lively and colorful.

Proper tool usage is crucial for effective plant care. Invest in a good pair of pruners with ergonomic handles that fit comfortably in your hand. Keep them clean and sharp to ensure precise cuts that heal quickly. Timing is everything; prune shrubs and perennials in early spring, while flowering plants benefit from regular deadheading throughout their bloom cycle. Remember, each snip is a step toward a healthier garden.

Plants, much like people, exhibit signs of stress when something isn't right. Wilting leaves might suggest underwatering, while yellowing could indicate nutrient deficiencies or root problems. It's essential to observe these signals and respond promptly. For wilting, check soil moisture and adjust your watering schedule accordingly. If leaves yellow, consider adding a balanced fertilizer to replenish lost nutrients. Compost or organic fertilizers work wonders here, providing the essential elements plants need to thrive.

Routine observation plays a pivotal role in maintaining plant health. A quick daily check allows you to spot potential issues before they escalate. Inspect leaves for signs of pests like aphids or spider mites. These tiny invaders can wreak havoc if left unchecked, but a simple spray of water or insecticidal soap often resolves the issue. Regular monitoring also helps you notice positive changes—new growth, budding flowers, or vibrant colors—which is incredibly rewarding.

The benefits of these practices extend beyond aesthetics; they contribute to the overall well-being of your garden. Healthy plants are more resilient to pests and diseases, and they produce more abundant blooms and fruits. By dedicating a few moments each day to plant care, you cultivate a garden that not only looks beautiful but also thrives with life and energy.

As you hone your skills in pruning and deadheading, remember that gardening is an evolving process. Each plant has its own rhythm and preferences, so stay curious and attentive to their needs. Don't hesitate to experiment with different techniques or schedules—what works for one plant might not suit another.

In this chapter, we've explored essential plant care techniques that form the foundation of a flourishing garden. From shaping with pruning to encouraging blooms through deadheading, these practices empower you to nurture healthy plants that enrich your space. As you continue your gardening journey, keep these insights in mind and embrace the joy of tending to your green companions.

In our next chapter, we'll delve into watering techniques and strategies for maintaining optimal soil moisture—a crucial aspect of container gardening success. Until then, enjoy the time spent with your plants and the small victories that come with each new leaf or flower.

CHAPTER 3
WATERING AND FERTILIZING ESSENTIALS

MASTERING THE ART OF WATERING: TECHNIQUES FOR BUSY SCHEDULES

Picture this: you're juggling work assignments, managing family commitments, and carving out some precious me-time, yet you persist in nurturing a dream of a flourishing container garden. The palpable challenge remains: how do you ensure your plants stay happy and healthy without dedicating copious amounts of time each day? The secret lies in adopting efficient and effective watering techniques specifically tailored for those with bustling and hectic lifestyles, without sacrificing the vitality of your garden. One remarkably effective method is the utilization of a drip irrigation system.

A drip irrigation setup delivers water directly to the base of each plant through a network of tubing and emitters, minimizing waste and ensuring consistent moisture. A small pump, often placed inside a water reservoir, pushes water through connected tubing up to the drip line, which runs above or alongside the containers. Emitters positioned above each pot release water slowly, providing efficient hydration directly to the roots. The system can be automated with a timer.

This savvy setup automates the entire watering process, which could be revolutionary for anyone who struggles to keep up with daily watering demands, providing the freedom to attend to life's myriad other obligations with ease. With essential components like emitters and tubing, this method allows you to customize the flow to meet the unique needs of each plant, ensuring optimal hydration even when you are not physically present to tend to them.

In addition to technological solutions, employing nature-inspired strategies can also enhance your watering regimen. For example, another invaluable strategy includes the introduction of moisture-retaining mulch. This cost-effective and straightforward solution greatly aids in helping the soil retain water, thereby reducing the frequency and intensity of watering required. Mulch acts like a protective shield or blanket, covering the soil surface to dramatically minimize evaporation. Options such as straw, bark chips, or even coconut coir not only trap moisture but also contribute additional nutrients to the soil as they decompose, thereby enriching the overall soil quality over time. By simply spreading a generous layer around your plants, you'll observe that they remain moist for prolonged periods, even during the most oppressive heat spells.

Commitment to consistent watering schedules is yet another cornerstone of sound plant health management. Establishing regular reminders or leveraging technology through apps can aid significantly in maintaining regularity. By doing so, you successfully mitigate the risks associated with both overwatering and underwatering. Many contemporary gardening apps provide features such as local weather forecasts and personalized alerts, keeping you informed about the best times to water your garden. Installing sensors to monitor soil moisture levels supplies additional real-time insight and precision, as these compact devices measure the soil's moisture content and alert you when it's time for another round of watering. They eliminate guesswork from the equation, permitting you to center your efforts on simply enjoying the vibrant oasis that is your green space.

Hot weather scenarios introduce unique challenges, but with some foresight and preparation, you can masterfully keep your plants hydrated even through the most torrid heat waves. Engaging in watering sessions early in the morning or late in the afternoon effectively minimizes evaporation, ensuring the roots can absorb maximum moisture for sustained nourishment.

Recognizing and interpreting the signs of water stress is critical for promptly troubleshooting any potential issues that may arise. Wilting leaves often indicate inadequate water supply, but they may also be symptomatic of root complications if the plant does not recover post-watering. Similarly, yellowing leaves may suggest overwatering, nutrient deficiencies, or other concerns, indicating that an adjustment in your approach may be necessary. Taking meticulous note of these symptoms allows for quick, responsive action to effectively prevent any long-term detriment.

Understanding these indicators and intricacies empowers you to make well-informed, confident decisions regarding your garden's needs. By refining your watering techniques, embracing technology while honoring natural methods, and being astutely attuned to signs of stress, you'll nurture a robust and thriving container garden that seamlessly integrates into your busy lifestyle. Gardening is truly about harmonizing different aspects of life— between work obligations and leisure activities, between attentive care and negligence. Equipped with these strategies and insights, you're poised to cultivate a vibrant garden that not only flourishes but stands as a testament to your dedication, adaptability, and passion for finding beauty amidst the chaos of life. Each plant speaks volumes of your steadfast commitment, thriving under the attentive care you provide.

SELF-WATERING CONTAINERS: A TIME-SAVING SOLUTION

Self-watering containers reduce the frequency of watering, allowing you more time to enjoy the garden rather than maintaining it. By ensuring consistent moisture levels, these containers create a stable environment for plant roots, minimizing stress. This consistency means that even when life gets hectic, your plants stay happy and hydrated. These containers are a game-changer, especially for those who want a lush garden without the commitment of daily upkeep.

Choosing the right self-watering system is paramount to achieving these benefits. Several types are available, each with its own strengths. Wick-based systems use a simple fabric wick that draws water from a reservoir at the bottom of the container into the soil above. This method is effective for smaller plants and herbs that require steady moisture. Reservoir-based containers feature a built-in water reservoir beneath the soil layer. Water seeps upward through capillary action, providing uniform moisture distribution. Capillary action systems work similarly but use a specialized mat or layer that allows water to rise from below, keeping the soil evenly moist. Understanding these options helps you select a system that aligns with your garden's needs and your lifestyle.

Setting up a self-watering container may initially seem complex, but it's quite straightforward with a little guidance. Start by assembling the container according to the instructions provided, ensuring each component fits securely. Most models require positioning a reservoir at the base with an overflow hole to prevent excess water buildup. Fill this reservoir with water and place the soil on top, embedding the wick or mat to draw moisture upward. The key here is ensuring that the wick maintains contact with both water and soil for effective functioning. Regular maintenance involves checking and refilling the reservoir as needed, typically every couple of weeks. Cleaning is equally essential to prevent algae growth, which can clog systems and impede water flow. Empty the reservoir periodically and scrub it with mild soap, rinsing thoroughly before refilling.

While self-watering containers offer numerous advantages, they aren't without their quirks. Algae growth in reservoirs is a common issue, but can be managed by keeping the reservoir covered or using opaque materials to limit sunlight exposure, which fuels algae proliferation. Proper drainage is another crucial aspect; without it, plants risk becoming waterlogged, leading to root rot. Ensure excess water can escape through designated drainage holes and consider adding a layer of coarse material like gravel at the bottom to facilitate drainage. Address these concerns proactively, and self-watering systems will provide reliable support for your garden's hydration needs.

The beauty of self-watering containers lies in their capacity to adapt to various gardening situations and plant types. Whether you're cultivating herbs on a sunny windowsill or growing tomatoes on the patio, these containers simplify care routines while promoting robust plant development. You'll experience fewer watering mishaps, as plants receive just the right amount of moisture, preventing both underwatering and overwatering. As you integrate self-watering systems into your gardening practice, you'll discover newfound freedom and flexibility in how you manage your green space.

Embracing self-watering technology gives you the confidence to explore more diverse plant species without being tethered to a rigid watering schedule. It opens doors to experimenting with delicate plants that demand constant moisture or expanding your garden during peak summer months when maintaining hydration becomes challenging. These systems act as silent partners in your gardening endeavors—reliable allies that ensure your plants flourish while you focus on other priorities.

Incorporating self-watering containers into your gardening toolkit offers more than just convenience; it transforms how you interact with your plants, fostering an environment where they can thrive independently of constant attention. With these systems in place, you'll find yourself spending less time troubleshooting watering issues and more time enjoying the verdant beauty that surrounds you.

CHOOSING THE RIGHT FERTILIZER: ORGANIC VS. SYNTHETIC

In the world of container gardening, choosing the right fertilizer is like picking the right fuel for your car. It directly impacts how well your plants grow and thrive. Let's delve into the differences between organic and synthetic fertilizers, so you can make informed choices. Organic fertilizers, derived from natural sources like compost and manure, release nutrients slowly over time. This gradual release feeds plants steadily, reducing the risk of nutrient leaching and promoting sustainable growth. On the other hand, synthetic fertilizers offer a quick nutrient boost, ideal for plants needing immediate attention. They are manufactured from minerals and chemicals, providing a precise nutrient balance that acts fast. However, this rapid release can sometimes lead to nutrient runoff, impacting the environment negatively. The choice between slow and fast nutrient release depends on your plants' needs and how quickly you want to see results.

Environmental impact is another factor to consider. Organic fertilizers enhance soil health by stimulating beneficial microorganisms and improving soil structure. They contribute to long-term soil fertility and reduce the risk of chemical buildup. Synthetic fertilizers, while effective, can leave residues that might alter soil chemistry over time and potentially harm local waterways through runoff. For eco-conscious gardeners, organic options often align better with sustainable practices.

Selecting the right fertilizer involves matching nutrients to plant needs. For leafy greens like lettuce and spinach, high-nitrogen fertilizers are ideal as they promote lush foliage growth. Look for organic options like fish emulsion or blood meal for a steady nitrogen supply. When it comes to flowering plants or those producing fruits, phosphorus-rich fertilizers work wonders. They support robust root development and enhance bloom quality. Bone meal or rock phosphate are excellent organic choices, providing a gentle phosphorus boost without overwhelming the plant.

Application methods play a crucial role in fertilizer effectiveness. Granular fertilizers are easy to apply and release nutrients slowly as you water your plants. They are great for long-term feeding but require even distribution across the soil surface. Liquid fertilizers offer immediate results, ideal for plants needing a quick nutrient uptake. They are easy to mix with water and apply during regular watering sessions. Foliar feeding is another technique where you spray diluted fertilizer directly onto leaves for rapid absorption. This method is especially useful if you notice signs of nutrient deficiencies like yellowing leaves or stunted growth.

Timing is everything when applying fertilizers. Early morning or late afternoon applications help avoid nutrient evaporation in hot weather. For most container plants, a bi-weekly schedule works well, but adjust based on plant response and growth stage. Young seedlings may need less frequent feeding compared to mature plants actively producing fruits or flowers.

Avoiding over-fertilization is key to maintaining plant health. Excess nutrients can lead to leaf burn—a condition where leaf edges turn brown and crispy due to salt buildup from fertilizers. This stress not only affects aesthetics but also reduces overall plant vigor. Soil testing is a valuable tool for preventing over-fertilization. Simple kits available at garden centers provide insights into nutrient levels, helping you tailor fertilizer applications accordingly.

Understanding these nuances in fertilizer choice and application empowers you to nurture healthy, vibrant container gardens that flourish season after season. Balancing between organic and synthetic options allows you to customize care based on your gardening goals and environmental considerations. As you experiment with different fertilizers, observe how your plants respond and adjust your approach as needed, creating a harmonious relationship between nutrients and plant growth.

By embracing this approach, you'll develop an intuitive sense of what your garden needs at different stages, leading to thriving plants that reflect your care and attention to detail. With each application, you're not just feeding plants; you're fostering a lively ecosystem that rewards your efforts with beauty and bounty.

FEEDING YOUR PLANTS: NUTRIENT NEEDS AT DIFFERENT GROWTH STAGES

Understanding the nutrient needs of your plants as they grow is like learning the language of your garden. From the moment a seedling breaks through the soil to the time it matures into a robust plant, its nutritional requirements shift. Initially, as roots begin to develop, a higher phosphorus content is crucial. Phosphorus strengthens root systems, setting a solid foundation for the plant to thrive. As plants grow, their needs change. When it's time for fruit and flower production, potassium takes center stage. Potassium supports the development of blooms and fruits, ensuring they are healthy and abundant. This nutrient balance is critical throughout the plant's life cycle.

Creating a feeding schedule tailored to your plants is essential for keeping them healthy and productive. Fast-growing vegetables like tomatoes or peppers benefit from weekly feeding. This consistent nutrient supply supports their rapid growth and high energy demands. In contrast, slower-growing herbs such as thyme or rosemary do well with monthly feedings. These plants require less frequent nutrition boosts, allowing them to develop at their own pace without becoming overwhelmed by excess nutrients. Adjusting your feeding routine based on plant type and growth rate ensures that each plant receives the right amount of care.

Micronutrients, though needed in smaller quantities, play a significant role in plant health. Iron, for instance, is vital for chlorophyll production, the green pigment responsible for photosynthesis. Without iron, leaves may yellow, hindering the plant's ability to harness energy from sunlight. Magnesium also plays an essential role in photosynthesis by activating enzymes that facilitate energy transfer. Though these trace elements might seem minor, they are crucial for overall plant vitality. Ensuring your plants receive these micronutrients can make all the difference in their growth and resilience.

Sometimes, despite your best efforts, plants may show signs of nutrient deficiencies or excesses. Recognizing these signals is key to addressing issues before they escalate. Yellow leaves often indicate an iron deficiency. A simple iron supplement can correct this, restoring the plant's lush green color and vigor. Similarly, stunted growth may suggest a need for balanced fertilizers that provide a spectrum of nutrients. By being observant and responsive to these signs, you can tweak nutrient levels to suit your plants' needs better.

REFLECTION SECTION: TRACKING PLANT HEALTH

Keeping a garden journal can be invaluable in monitoring your plants' nutrient needs over time. Jot down observations about leaf color, growth rates, and any changes you notice after feeding. Note any adjustments made to your fertilizing routine and their outcomes. This practice not only helps track progress but also builds a wealth of personalized knowledge about your garden's unique requirements.

By embracing this understanding of nutrient needs throughout different growth stages, you empower yourself to cultivate a thriving container garden that flourishes season after season.

Balancing macro and micronutrients while adjusting feeding schedules based on plant health creates an environment where your plants can truly prosper.

Incorporating these insights into your gardening practice enriches your connection with nature and deepens your appreciation for the intricate dance of growth and nourishment that sustains life in your containers.

WATER CONSERVATION STRATEGIES FOR ECO-CONSCIOUS GARDENERS

Imagine walking into your garden, surrounded by lush greens and vibrant blooms, knowing with immense satisfaction that you're playing an active role in preserving our precious planet's resources. Water conservation is not merely a fashionable catchphrase or transient trend; rather, it's an essential practice imbued with profound significance, particularly for those among us with an acute awareness of our environmental impact. By employing simple yet effective strategies, we can make a significant difference.

One remarkably efficient method of conserving water involves the use of rainwater barrels. This environmentally-friendly and budget-conscious approach is as practical as it is ingenious. Visualize, if you will, strategically placing these barrels beneath your home's downspouts, where they discreetly yet effectively collect rainwater. During the dry spells, this reserve of rainwater stands ready to invigorate your garden, offering life-giving hydration without dipping into precious tap water reserves. Not only is this practice conducive to water saving, but it also furnishes your garden with natural, untreated water that is rich in nutrients and often more beneficial for plant health compared to treated alternatives.

In your pursuit of water conservation, another highly beneficial approach is utilizing greywater systems. These ingenious systems allow for the recycling of water from household sources such as baths, sinks, and washing machines, repurposing it for irrigation needs within your garden. By installing a straightforward grey-water system, you open the door to reusing household water, which serves to cut down on water waste and optimize available resources. Engaging in such a project can be particularly rewarding if you have a penchant for DIY solutions. Bear in mind the wisdom of utilizing eco-friendly soaps and detergents, ensuring that this recycled water remains a boon to your plants, rather than a detriment.

When curating your garden's collection of flora, it is wise to take into consideration plants that flourish with minimal water. A perfect inclusion to your environmentally mindful garden would be succulents and cacti, known for their natural ability to withstand arid climates. Their thick, fleshy leaves act as reservoirs, storing water and enabling survival even under harsh, dry conditions. Additionally, consider the inclusion of native plants—species that have adapted perfectly to your local climate and require minimal additional watering. These plants, steeped in the wisdom of adaptation, effortlessly navigate the vacillations of your region's weather patterns. In doing so, they not only bolster your water conservation efforts but also inject an array of vivid textures and hues into your garden's aesthetic.

Mulching, an age-old gardening practice, emerges as a reliable ally in the campaign for water conservation. By enveloping the soil with a protective layer of organic mulch, such as straw or wood chips, you effectively reduce evaporation rates and maintain ideal soil moisture levels. This practice ensures longer periods of hydration for your garden while reducing the need for frequent watering. The added benefit is the gradual improvement of soil health over time. Alternatively, inorganic options like gravel or pebbles might catch your fancy, offering a sleek, modern aesthetic and keeping both weeds and moisture levels in balance.

Amplifying your efforts through community involvement can have a dramatic impact on your conservation journey. Consider joining or even initiating local gardening groups that are driven by the shared pursuit of sustainability. Such initiatives foster community spirit and a collective sense of accountability. Within these groups, you may discover fellow gardening enthusiasts who share your passion for environmentally friendly practices and can exchange invaluable tips and resources with you. Community gardens are often epicenters of sustainable practices, featuring shared composting facilities and rainwater collection systems, contributing to collective conservation aims while encouraging social connectivity.

Adopting these water conservation strategies not only serves to enrich the environment but also enables the cultivation of a more sustainable garden. Through the embrace of these thoughtful practices, your garden can thrive without demanding excessive water usage. This harmonious balance reflects an alignment with both the garden's needs and the Earth's resources. Your garden then becomes a sanctuary symbolizing beauty and responsibility, embodying the nurturing of plants and the earth alike.

As you explore and incorporate these techniques, you'll soon come to realize that conservation transcends simply saving water. It morphs into the creation of a resilient ecosystem capable of flourishing with minimal human intervention. By embracing these methodologies within your gardening routine, know that each step you take is a contribution to the well-being of your plants and our planet.

TROUBLESHOOTING WATERING ISSUES: OVERWATERING AND UNDERWATERING

Navigating the balance between overwatering and underwatering can feel like learning a new language, but it's essential for the health of your container plants. Overwatering can lead to root rot, a condition where the roots can't function properly due to excess moisture. This often manifests as yellow, droopy leaves that paradoxically make the plant appear thirsty. On the flip side, underwatering causes the soil to dry out and pull away from the container's sides, while leaves become dry and brittle. Both scenarios stress the plant, but with careful observation and adjustment, you can learn to maintain the perfect moisture level for your container garden.

Addressing these watering missteps, whether rooted in excess or scarcity, requires decisive and thoughtful action. Should overwatering be the primary culprit, transforming your pot's soil blend is essential. Incorporate elements such as perlite or sand to enhance drainage, aerating the soil to prohibit water accumulation. Introduce these amendments gradually, adjusting the soil's composition until it fosters a balance between moisture retention and aeration. For those chronically underwatered plants, establishing a habitual watering routine is crucial. Employ the simple yet effective method of soil moisture testing—gently insert your finger into the soil to about an inch depth, evaluating its need for water. If the soil clings with moisture, resist the urge to water; if not, provide your plant the hydration it craves. This finger-test, casual yet immensely effective, allows you to tailor the water schedule specifically to each plant's needs, recognizing that one schedule does not fit all.

The adverse effects of persistent watering issues extend beyond the superficial aesthetics of drooping leaves. Unchecked, they can severely impact a plant's vitality, reducing its ability to bloom or bear fruit. Plants under stress from inadequate watering are akin to warriors weakened in the heat of battle, their defenses lowered, rendering them susceptible to pest invasions and diseases. This vulnerability can be likened to the human experience of battling illnesses while dehydrated—the body's barriers compromised, its fight significantly harder. Providing plants with an optimal balance of care—moisture, air, and nutrients—ensures they maintain their inherent protective abilities, warding off potential invaders.

To prevent future watering dilemmas, adopt the habit of vigilant monitoring. Regular assessments of soil moisture can preempt many common issues before they manifest. Develop the practice of adjusting your watering strategy as needed, an informed response to the subtle shifts in environmental conditions and plant growth. Maintaining a detailed watering log can be immensely beneficial—record each watering event, noting time, quantity, and any observed plant responses. Over time, this simple practice becomes a goldmine of data, revealing patterns and facilitating informed decisions to tweak and improve your care regimen.

As we draw this chapter to a close, we appreciate the intricate role that proper watering plays in successful container gardening. Beyond mere hydration, it involves creating conducive conditions where plants can flourish unabated. Mastering these watering techniques translates into healthier, more resilient plants, resulting in a thriving garden that resists pests, disease, and unfurls magnificent blossoms and fruits. Armed with these strategies, you are well-prepared to nurture a lush container garden, transforming your environment with beauty and vibrancy.

Next, we will delve into the art and science of designing your container garden layout for visual and functional brilliance. With your newfound understanding of watering behind you, embark on this next journey—curating a living masterpiece that truly reflects your personal style and creative vision.

CHAPTER 4
DESIGNING YOUR CONTAINER GARDEN

VERTICAL GARDENING: UTILIZING HEIGHT IN SMALL SPACES

P icture yourself standing on your tiny balcony, surrounded by lush greenery that climbs upwards, ambitiously defying gravity and transforming what was once an empty, unembellished wall into a lively vertical paradise. Vertical gardening represents not merely a practical solution for spatial constraints but also an artistic endeavor that adds rich layers of life and aesthetic beauty to your garden. Growing upwards allows you to maximize the potential of your available footprint, thereby making room for a greater abundance of plants than you might have envisaged possible. This method not only optimizes your usage of space but drastically enhances the visual appeal of the area by introducing depth and texture to your surroundings. The vertical element inherently draws one's eye upward, bestowing a sense of grandeur and expansiveness even in the smallest of spaces, creating an optical illusion of a more substantial garden.

Example of a vertical garden

Moreover, the benefits of vertical gardening extend beyond mere aesthetics. Elevating plants away from the ground reduces their exposure to soil-borne diseases and pests, allowing for better airflow around the foliage and stems of the plants. As a result, your plants can grow healthier and more robustly. Furthermore, the act of harvesting becomes a delightful breeze as fruits and vegetables conveniently dangle within easy reach, sparing you the need to crouch, bend, or stoop awkwardly. Popular systems for vertical gardening include trellises, wall planters, and hanging baskets.

Each presents distinct advantages suitable for varying space constraints and specific gardening needs.

The process of constructing vertical supports can be an immensely rewarding DIY project, or it might simply be an effortless trip to your local gardening store, contingent on your preference. For those inclined towards the handiwork of do-it-yourself projects, bamboo stakes, creatively bound with twine, make for excellent trellises. They stand firm, offer a natural aesthetic, and are wonderfully affordable. Additionally, recycling materials, such as old ladders or wooden pallets, can stimulate creativity and provide unique plant supports. Store-bought options, on the other hand, afford considerable convenience and a wide array of choices; wall planters, made in metal or plastic, simplify installation and maintenance very efficiently, serving well for herbs or flowers requiring shallow soil.

When choosing plants for a vertical garden, consider those species that naturally climb or trail. Ideal candidates include climbing plants like peas and beans, as they naturally seek upward support, making them organically suitable for trellises, and they produce substantial, fulfilling harvests. Their tendrils adeptly latch onto structures, which facilitates an easy training process along trellis work. Trailing plants such as nasturtiums spill forth vibrant blooms over the edges of planters, bringing splashes of vivid color and delightful charm, all while requiring minimal maintenance yet providing high-impact, visual results.

Maintaining a vertical garden calls for thoughtful attention to detail, but is far from overwhelming or daunting. Regular pruning is instrumental, as it promotes upward growth and aids in sustaining a neat and structured appearance. It is vital to remove any damaged or crowded leaves to improve light penetration, enhance air circulation, and foster healthier growth. Proper irrigation is crucial; ensure consistent water distribution through tools like drip systems or soaker hoses that deliver moisture directly to the roots, optimizing water usage and plant health. It's essential to frequently monitor soil moisture, as elevated containers typically dry out faster than ground-level ones, requiring occasional adjustments to watering practices.

INTERACTIVE ELEMENT: VERTICAL GARDEN PLANNING EXERCISE

Engage in an exercise where you take time to sketch out your envisioned vertical garden layout. Consider your available wall space, railings, and other spots amenable to vertical structures. Think through your plant choices based on sunlight exposure—select climbers for those bright, sunny areas, while opting for shade-tolerant trailers suited for shadier spots. This brainstorming and sketching activity will help you visualize your space's full potential, enabling you to make more informed and strategic plant selections that best suit your garden environment.

Vertical gardening is an exploration of endless possibilities when it comes to creativity and productivity. It represents a novel approach of reimagining your space and challenging the conventional paradigms of gardening. Embrace the vertical dimension and witness as your garden experiences unprecedented growth and beauty, flourishing like never before, creating an environment that is both functionally optimal and visually stunning.

CREATING EYE-CATCHING ARRANGEMENTS: COLOR, TEXTURE, AND FORM

Crafting a visually stunning container garden involves more than just planting your favorite flowers. It's about understanding basic design principles, which transform your space from ordinary to extraordinary. Color, texture, and form are your allies in this artistic pursuit. Let's start with color. Imagine the color wheel as your palette. Colors opposite each other, like blue and orange, create vibrant contrast and energy, while colors adjacent to each other, such as red and pink, offer harmony and subtlety. These combinations can evoke different moods. Warm colors like reds and yellows energize, while cool hues like blues and purples provide calm. By playing with these shades, you can shape your garden's atmosphere to reflect the feeling you want to evoke.

Texture adds another layer of interest to your arrangements. Mixing textures is like combining different fabrics in fashion; it creates depth and intrigue. Pair coarse-textured plants like lamb's ear or dusty miller with finer textures such as ferns or grasses. This contrast allows each plant to stand out, enhancing its individual characteristics. Texture isn't just about leaves; it includes stem shapes and the surfaces of flowers, too. Variegated leaves, which display multiple colors or patterns, are another way to introduce texture and visual interest. They break up monotony and draw the eye, adding complexity without overwhelming the arrangement.

Effective plant combinations bring these elements together seamlessly. Consider mixing bold foliage with delicate blooms. For instance, large-leaf hostas paired with dainty impatiens create a striking balance between strength and grace. Variegated leaves can be the showstopper in a container filled with simpler plants. Imagine a pot where the star is a variegated coleus surrounded by soft white petunias. The leaves' patterns catch the light differently throughout the day, offering dynamic visual shifts as time passes.

Arranging containers for maximum impact involves more than just choosing plants; it's about how you display them. Creating focal points is key. Use height variations to draw attention and guide the eye naturally through the space. A tall ornamental grass in a central container can act as an anchor, while smaller pots filled with mounding flowers fan out around it. Group containers with similar themes for a cohesive look, or mix styles for an eclectic feel. Consider using containers of varying sizes and shapes to add rhythm and flow to your display.

Seasonal changes offer opportunities to refresh your garden's appeal. Introducing seasonal annuals provides bursts of fresh color throughout the year. In spring, try planting pansies for early cheerfulness, followed by summer's bright zinnias. As autumn sets in, replace these with chrysanthemums for rich, warm hues that echo the season's natural palette. Rotating plants keeps your garden dynamic and ensures that there's always something new to catch the eye. It also allows you to experiment with different plant combinations each season.

Finally, remember that gardening is an ongoing conversation between you and your plants. You learn their language as you observe how they respond to different conditions and combinations. Adjust and adapt based on what you see—some plants might thrive together while others need more space or different care. Your garden becomes a reflection of your evolving tastes and understanding, a living canvas that changes with each choice you make.

Incorporate these principles into your container gardening practice to create arrangements that are not only beautiful but also meaningful. Each element—color, texture, form—contributes to a tapestry that speaks to both the heart and senses, inviting you to engage more deeply with your environment.

DIY CONTAINER PROJECTS: UPCYCLING AND CREATIVE SOLUTIONS

Envision looking around your living space, identifying unused items, and picturing them reborn as distinctive planters, each boasting its own unique appeal. Upcycling turns mundane objects into eye-catching elements, infusing both character and eco-friendliness into your gardening space. By repurposing different items, you not only give them a new lease on life but also reimagine their purpose and value creatively.

Let's first consider old tires. Often discarded without a second thought, these resilient rubber structures hold potential far beyond their original use. When stacked or painted, they can become bold, eye-catching planters that draw the admiration of onlookers. The inherent sturdiness of tires makes them robust containers suitable for accommodating larger plants or even small shrubs. By drilling several drainage holes and adding vibrant paint, these tires transform into colorful statement pieces, breathing new life into otherwise mundane corners of your yard or balcony. The durability of the tire material ensures these planters withstand the elements, offering longevity and enduring appeal for your green companions.

Wooden pallets offer another ingenious avenue for crafting vertical gardens. These commonly available structures can be repurposed into a lush tapestry of greenery mounted against your wall. To begin, sand them down to remove splinters and apply a weatherproof sealant, ensuring their outdoor resilience. Attaching small pots or fabric pockets along the slats, you create a tapestry of foliage, with each plant cascading downwards in a visual feast. This vertical arrangement not only optimizes space but also adds an inviting rustic charm to any environment. The natural texture and warmth of wood, combined with the vibrant life of herbs or flowers, create a harmonious and organic visual display that rejuvenates the senses.

For enthusiasts who enjoy a hands-on project, painting and sealing wooden crates can be an engaging and rewarding task. The key is to choose colors that harmonize with your garden's existing palette, employing non-toxic paints to guarantee safety for plants and the environment alike. Once painted, applying a waterproof sealant offers protection against moisture infiltration, extending the life of these delightful planters. The versatility of these crates adds layers of dynamism to any garden layout—stack them, line them up, place them at angles, or even hang them horizontally. This approach creates varying heights and structures, adding depth and interest to your garden's overall visual scheme.

Tin cans, often overlooked, hold potential for delightful transformation into quaint herb gardens with just a sprinkling of creativity. First, clean and strip the labels from the cans, then persistently use a hammer and nail to poke drainage holes in the bottom, ensuring proper water flow. Adding a coat of paint or decorative paper wraps elevates these simple objects into eye-catching containers, perfectly suited for windowsills or small ledges. Herbs like basil, mint, or rosemary thrive in these confined spaces, enjoying the warmth and nourishment provided within indoor environments. The beauty of a personalized container lies in its ability to reflect your unique style while engendering a positive environmental impact.

Finding materials for these projects requires little more than a keen eye and resourcefulness. Thrift stores offer a treasure trove of potential planters, each holding stories of past lives waiting to be discovered—old teapots, metal buckets, and woven baskets can all find newfound purposes within your garden. By joining local buy-nothing groups on social media platforms, you connect with a community of like-minded individuals eager to exchange items for free. Such exchanges open yet another avenue for sourcing materials at no cost, emphasizing community spirit and shared resourcefulness.

Engaging in upcycling projects fosters an essence of creativity, spurs sustainable living, and results in truly unique containers. Even the smallest space, with the aid of resourceful imaginations, transforms into a vibrant garden brimming with personality and character. By repurposing items in inventive ways, you not only aesthetically enhance your garden but also weave an intricate story —one of innovation, environmental care, and personalized flair.

DESIGNING WITH SUCCULENTS: LOW-MAINTENANCE BEAUTY

Step into a garden oasis that feels serene and tranquil, where every plant showcases resilience and adaptability. In this space, succulents shine as the stars of container gardening. They captivate both beginners and seasoned gardeners with their charm and robustness. Succulents are magical for their ability to thrive with minimal care, making them a perfect match for individuals with busy lives who might not always remember to water their plants. Their natural drought resistance means they're incredibly forgiving, ideal for those starting their gardening journey.

The dizzying variety of succulents further enhances their allure. From the soft, velvety texture of echeveria's intricately layered rosettes, which resemble delicate floral sculptures, to the robust, spiky allure of aloe with its medicinal prowess, succulents offer an eclectic mix of forms and hues. This diversity means you have an immense palette from which to craft a garden that isn't just visually enchanting but is a wholly personal expression of your aesthetic preferences and creativity.

When creating succulent arrangements, think of yourself as an artist with living plants as your medium. Each succulent is like a brushstroke, contributing to the overall beauty of your piece. For a striking composition, mix plants of different heights and shapes. For example, combine the tall, slender snake plants with the short, rounded hens and chicks. This variety creates an engaging visual journey. Adding decorative gravel or stones not only improves drainage but also enhances the aesthetic, giving your arrangement a refined, natural look. These touches mimic the succulents' native habitats, making your arrangement appear as though it's a slice of a sun-kissed desert brought into your home.

Caring for these resilient beauties is delightfully straightfor-ward, yet adhering to a few key guidelines will ensure that your succulents maintain their vibrant health and lush appearance. Para-mount among these is the selection of well-draining soil. Tradi-tional potting soil is notoriously moisture-retentive and thus unsuitable; instead, choose a sandy, gritty mix, potentially augmented with additional elements like perlite or pumice, specifi-cally designed for succulents and cacti. This eschews the peril of waterlogged roots, a common precursor to root rot—the arch-nemesis of succulents. Moreover, approaching watering with a philosophy of minimalism is essential: allow the soil to dry completely between drenchings, replicating the natural ebb and flow of dry conditions followed by infrequent, yet substantial, rainfall.

Succulents transcend the conventional confines of pots and planters, offering innovative display opportunities that infuse your living spaces with a dash of creative flair. Imagine the aesthetic possibilities of hanging succulent gardens, which are ideal for compact areas where horizontal surface area is scarce. Picture a vertical frame transformed into a living artwork, where vibrant succulents spill organically, evoking the beauty of wild cliffs or arboreal habitats. For a seasonal touch, a succulent wreath ingeniously offers a festive yet enduring alternative to traditional decor. By arranging tiny succulent cuttings within a circular design, supported by a sturdy wireframe and lush moss, you foster a dynamic centerpiece that morphs and grows over time, imbued with rustic charm and modern elegance.

The intrinsic charm of succulents is underscored by their effortless versatility and adaptability, rendering them the perfect choice for those desiring elegance without the encumbrance of intensive caretaking. The myriad forms, textures, and colors of succulents present you with limitless opportunities to unleash your creativity, enabling you to infuse your personal style into your environment while nurturing the serene tranquility that nature offers. Whether you're embarking on intricate crafts or venturing into novel displays, succulents provide an expansive canvas upon which your imagination can wander and innovate unfettered.

CREATING A POLLINATOR-FRIENDLY GARDEN IN CONTAINERS

Picture a vibrant garden, alive with the gentle hum of bees and the delicate flutter of butterfly wings; colorful blossoms sway gently in the breeze, painting your space with vivid hues and lively movement. This idyllic tableau isn't just a scene from a nature documentary—it's a pollinator-friendly garden right on your balcony or patio, crafted with intent and care. Pollinators, which include a diverse array of bees, butterflies, and even beetles, play an unquestionably crucial role in maintaining our ecosystem's integrity by facilitating the reproduction of plants through the transfer of pollen. Without these industrious creatures, our gardens, orchards, and even the broader food supply chain would face dire consequences. By enticing bees and butterflies to make your container garden their home, you not only enhance the beauty and productivity of your plant life but also make a valuable contribution to overall ecosystem health. These petite yet mighty creatures are pivotal in enhancing urban biodiversity, particularly in dense city areas where green spaces are often limited. They form essential pockets of life that provide sustenance not just to plants but to various wildlife forms intricately connected to these biological networks.

Choosing the right plants is paramount when it comes to captivating these industrious and beneficial insects. Take, for example, the enchanting lavender; its soothing, aromatic scent and delicate purple blooms act like a siren call for bees. Lavender flowers are rich in nectar, providing an irresistible treat that draws bees to your garden. Similarly, borage, with its striking star-shaped blue flowers, not only attracts bees with its nectar but also captivates the human eye with its vigorous and lively hue. For enthusiasts eager to support the mesmerizing monarch butterfly, the inclusion of milkweed in your garden is absolutely vital. Monarchs, in their enigmatic lifecycle, lay their eggs on milkweed plants, while their emerging caterpillars depend exclusively on the leaves for nourishment. This plant, therefore, not only sustains the monarch butterfly population but also infuses your space with a touch of wild, untamed beauty, reminiscent of vast meadows and thriving woodlands.

Designing a pollinator-friendly layout requires foresight and a holistic approach beyond merely selecting plants. It's about creating an ecosystem within your containers that invites, welcomes, and sustains tiny creatures. Start by layering your plants to provide a variety of access points that cater to different foraging habits. Taller plants, such as commanding sunflowers or majestic hollyhocks, offer shelter and strategic landing zones, while shorter plants like lavender and borage facilitate easy nectar access. This thoughtful plant layering echoes the natural stratification found in thriving landscapes, stimulating pollinators to explore various plant heights in their quest for sustenance. Integrate essential water sources as well—small, shallow dishes filled with pebbles can suffice, allowing pollinators to safely drink without the risk of drowning. These attentive touches transform your garden into a welcoming haven for visiting insects.

Maintaining a thriving pollinator habitat demands careful and thoughtful care. First and foremost, eschew the use of chemical pesticides that can inadvertently cause harm to pollinators. Numerous pesticides are toxic to bees and butterflies, disrupting their populations and hindering their pollination capabilities. Instead, embrace natural pest control methods that safeguard both your cherished plants and the vital insects that play their part in keeping your garden alive. Regular deadheading is a crucial ongoing task as well—by diligently removing spent blooms, you promote continuous flowering, ensuring that your garden remains an alluring spot for pollinators seeking nectar.

REFLECTION SECTION: POLLINATOR OBSERVATION JOURNAL

Embark on a reflective journey by starting a journal dedicated to observing the pollinators visiting your garden. Give notice to the multitude of species that grace your space, taking note of their preferred plants and any noticeable changes over time. This practice not only elevates your awareness of the indispensable role these creatures play but also deepens your understanding of how your garden nurtures and supports them. In time, this journal may become a treasured record of your garden's vibrancy and life.

Creating a pollinator-friendly garden transcends mere aesthetics; it is an invitation to give back to nature while immersing yourself in the breathtaking wonders of wildlife right at your doorstep. Watching bees buzz purposefully around lavender or delighting as butterflies perform an aerial ballet on milkweed evokes a profound sense of harmony and fulfillment that expands the joys of gardening into a form of stewardship and care for our shared environment. By consciously making these insightful choices, you play an integral role in sustaining the delicate balance of our natural world, all from the comfort and convenience of your own home.

INTEGRATING EDIBLES AND ORNAMENTALS FOR A FUNCTIONAL GARDEN

In envisioning a garden where aesthetics and functionality merge seamlessly, one imagines a place where beautiful blossoms and verdant leaves mix effortlessly with edible plants, creating a landscape that is not only pleasing to the eye but also fruitful in yield. This is the art and magic of mixed planting—a strategic approach to gardening that brings together the edible and the ornamental within your garden containers. This method does more than just optimize the limited space gardeners often face; it transforms your garden into a vivid and lively tapestry of colors, textures, and fragrances. By integrating both ornamental and edible plants, you cultivate an environment where every plant plays a crucial role in contributing to the overall utility and visual charm of your outdoor space.

Mixed gardens are significantly more than merely a visual delight. They offer numerous practical benefits that enhance and enrich your gardening journey. For instance, marigolds, when planted next to tomatoes, serve as natural pest deterrents, especially against aphids, thanks to their innate ability to repel various insects. This simple yet effective companion planting not only keeps your tomato plants healthier and free from pest infestations, but it also adorns your garden with brilliant bursts of orange, strikingly contrasting with the lush green foliage and deep red of the tomatoes. Likewise, the inclusion of basil next to petunias introduces a fresh and enticing aroma to your garden ambiance while simultaneously boosting its aesthetic appeal, courtesy of the vibrant hues of petunia blossoms. Furthermore, the robust fragrance of basil acts as a natural insect repellent, ensuring that your garden prospers with vitality.

Crafting and planning a mixed garden layout necessitates strategic thought and foresight to guarantee that each plant is situated in an environment conducive to its growth, receiving the optimal amount of sunlight and water. Begin by thoroughly assessing the individual needs of each plant species. More often than not, edible plants require full sun exposure to ensure ample production, whereas certain ornamental species flourish best in partially shaded conditions. Striking a balance between these requirements involves situating sun-loving varieties in the most sunlight-rich areas and allocating shaded spots for those that thrive with lesser direct sunlight exposure. Proper spacing is of paramount importance, as densely packed plants will vigorously vie for resources, potentially hampering their growth and development. Ensure there is adequate space for each plant to mature and expand without infringing upon the territory of nearby plants.

Sustaining a mixed garden effectively involves attending to the diverse and specific needs of different plant types. Edibles usually demand a higher intake of nutrients compared to ornamentals, making regular feedings an essential practice. Apply a balanced fertilizer consistently to maintain their health, vigor, and productivity throughout the growing season. Simultaneously, be vigilant with your ornamental plants, pruning them periodically to circumvent overcrowding and to improve air circulation. This essential maintenance not only elevates the visual appeal of your garden but also mitigates the likelihood of disease outbreaks.

REFLECTION EXERCISE: MIXED GARDEN PLANNING

Picture your ultimate mixed garden, taking into consideration which edibles and ornamentals you envision growing together. Draft a rough sketch of your layout, contemplating how these plants complement and enhance one another aesthetically and functionally. This introspective exercise in planning will aid you in strategically mapping out your garden, ensuring that each plant is positioned in a spot where it can thrive to its fullest potential.

Incorporating both edibles and ornamentals into your container garden offers a unique blend of aesthetic beauty and practicality. This harmonious combination means you can savor the joys of fresh produce ready for harvest while enjoying breathtaking blooms that augment your home's curb appeal. Through thoughtful planning and diligent care, one can cultivate a balanced and synergistic environment that offers delight and sustenance in equal measure, bestowing joy and nourishment upon your daily life.

As we conclude this chapter, let us contemplate how the blending of diverse plant types can enhance both the productivity and visual allure of your garden. It is about establishing harmony and synergy within your space, allowing you to embrace and relish the abundance of nature on multiple levels. In the subsequent chapter, we will explore methods and techniques to nurture healthy growth across a variety of plant species, ensuring your container garden remains vibrant and flourishing through the changing seasons.

MAKE A DIFFERENCE WITH YOUR REVIEW

A SMALL ACT CAN GROW BIG THINGS

"The meaning of life is to plant trees under whose shade you do not expect to sit." – Nelson Henderson

People who help others without asking for anything in return are some of the happiest folks around. So here's a way you can make a difference!

There are tons of people out there who want to grow their own food or flowers but don't know where to begin. Sound familiar?

That's why I wrote *The Ultimate Beginner's Guide to Container*

Gardening. But here's the thing: I can only reach new readers with your help.

Most people look at reviews before picking a book. If you leave a review, even a short one, it could help someone else take that first step.

Your review could inspire...

- one more neighbor to grow their own fresh herbs,
- one more balcony to fill with blooming flowers,
- one more kid to fall in love with gardening,
- one more family to start eating what they grow,
- one more person to find peace through plants.

Writing a review takes less than a minute, but it could mean the world to someone else. **Just scan the QR or follow this link:**

https://www.amazon.com/review/review-your-purchases/?asin=B0F8KB1V1L

If you love helping people grow—plants and all—then you're my kind of person. Thank you so much for being part of this gardening journey.

Avery Sage

CHAPTER 5
DEALING WITH PESTS AND DISEASES

IDENTIFYING COMMON PESTS IN CONTAINER GARDENS

As you embark on your container gardening adventure, there's nothing more disheartening than discovering your flourishing plants under siege by tiny invaders. Picture this: you're admiring your vibrant greens, only to notice some leaves turning yellow and others looking a bit stunted. Your initial joy at seeing new growth is quickly replaced by a sense of foreboding—a sense that something is amiss. Welcome to the world of pest challenges in container gardening, where even the smallest critters can wreak havoc if left unchecked. Like silent marauders, these pests descend upon your garden, threatening the health and vitality of your cherished plants.

Consider two prevalent pests: aphids and spider mites. Aphids, small insects that feast on plant sap, vary in color, including shades of green, black, and white. These pests typically gather on new growth or beneath leaf surfaces, appearing as if marshaling for an onslaught. Aphids drain the sap from your plants, leaving a sticky substance known as honeydew in their wake. This residue is not only unsightly but also cultivates sooty mold, a fungal disease that cloaks leaves in a black, powdery film, obstructing vital sunlight. In contrast, spider mites are nearly invisible critters that create thin webbing around plants, causing leaves to exhibit a speckled or bronzed appearance when infested.

Recognizing the signs of these uninvited guests is crucial. Yellowing leaves, stunted growth, or visible insects on stems and leaves are clear indicators. Sometimes, the signs are subtle, whispering rather than screaming, yet they are no less significant. Inspect your plants closely—initial damage may not always be immediately obvious. That's where a magnifying glass becomes your best friend, helping you spot these tiny pests early. It illuminates a hidden world where these diminutive creatures carry out their destructive work. Turn over leaves regularly; pests often hide there, laying eggs or munching away unnoticed, like saboteurs in the night.

Monitoring your plants is like a regular check-up at the doctor's—essential for maintaining health. Think of it as a routine health examination for your verdant patients. Make it a habit to inspect your plants every few days, a gentle nudge that encourages you to stay connected with your garden. Use a magnifying glass for detailed inspections and gently turn leaves to check for eggs or larvae. This close inspection ensures that nothing escapes your notice. Early detection is key; catching pest issues early prevents them from spreading to neighboring plants and reduces the need for intensive treatments. Like a prudent guardian, you are preempting potential disasters, ensuring that your plants remain strong and resilient.

The importance of early detection cannot be overstated. It's the difference between a minor inconvenience and a full-blown infestation. By nipping problems in the bud, you protect not only the affected plant but also its neighbors from potential harm. This proactive approach saves you from resorting to heavy-duty measures later on. It's a strategic defense, a way of safeguarding your garden's future health and vitality.

Visual Element: Pest Identification Chart

Common Garden Pests

	Aphid	Tiny, pear-shaped insects (green, black, or yellow). Found clustered under leaves; they suck plant sap.
	Whitefly	Small, white, moth-like insects. Flutter up in clouds when disturbed; feed on underside of leaves
	Spider Mite	Extremely small, red or yellow. Leave behind fine webbing; cause stippling or yellowing of leaves
	Cabbage Worm	Green caterpillars that chew large holes in cabbage-family plants. Often blend in with
	Cutworm	Fat, gray or brown caterpillars. Hide in soil and cut young seedlings off at the base during

This handy reference can help you quickly identify any unwelcome visitors in your garden. Keep this chart in your gardening toolkit, your horticultural playbook against the forces of destruction. With a quick glance, you'll be able to assess threats and plan your response.

Remember, dealing with pests is part of gardening. It's a learning experience that strengthens your skills as a gardener. Like a chess player who learns from every move, you will become more adept at predicting and countering every threat. With vigilance and care, you can keep these pesky intruders at bay and ensure your container garden remains healthy and vibrant. Each challenge faced and overcome is a testament to your growth as a gardener, a reminder that the wonders of nature come with their own set of trials. But with perseverance and knowledge, you will prevail.

NATURAL PEST CONTROL: ECO-FRIENDLY SOLUTIONS THAT WORK

In the realm of container gardening, maintaining a healthy garden without relying on harsh chemicals is not only possible but preferable. Enter the world of natural pest control methods, where you can keep those pesky critters at bay while nurturing a safe environment for both you and the planet. Neem oil stands out as a helpful resource, particularly against soft-bodied insects like aphids. This oil, derived from the seeds of the neem tree, acts as a natural pesticide, disrupting the life cycle of these pests. When aphids feast on plants treated with neem oil, they ingest compounds that interfere with their ability to grow and reproduce. The beauty of neem oil lies in its specificity; it targets pests without harming beneficial insects like bees or ladybugs. It's a bit like having a security system that knows exactly who to let through and who to keep out.

Another effective method is using diatomaceous earth. This powdery substance is made from the fossilized remains of tiny aquatic organisms called diatoms. When sprinkled around your plants, it forms a barrier that deters crawling pests such as slugs and snails. As these pests crawl over the diatomaceous earth, the sharp edges of the particles damage their exoskeletons, leading to dehydration and ultimately their demise. It's a bit like walking barefoot over broken glass—unpleasant and something to be avoided. What makes diatomaceous earth particularly appealing is its non-toxic nature, ensuring that it poses no risk to your pets or family members. And since it's just crushed fossils, it's completely biodegradable, making it environmentally friendly as well.

Natural pest control methods offer numerous benefits beyond just a pest-free garden. They are safe for humans and pets, meaning you won't have to worry about harmful residues on your plants or in your home. Imagine being able to pluck a ripe tomato straight from the vine and pop it into your mouth without a second thought about chemical contamination. That's the peace of mind natural methods provide. In addition, these solutions contribute to environmental sustainability by reducing reliance on synthetic chemicals that can leach into the soil and waterways. You're not just protecting your plants; you're also playing a part in preserving the ecosystem.

Implementing these natural solutions is straightforward, even for beginner gardeners. To apply neem oil, mix two teaspoons of neem oil with a quart of water and a few drops of dish soap to help the mixture adhere to leaves. Pour this into a spray bottle and douse your plants, focusing on affected areas. The dish soap acts as an emulsifier, allowing the oil and water to mix effectively. For diatomaceous earth, simply dust it over leaves and around plant bases, forming an invisible fortress against intruders. This fine powder can be gently applied with a soft brush or shaken from a duster for even distribution.

While natural methods are highly effective, they do come with their own set of challenges. Ensuring thorough coverage is crucial for success; missing spots can allow pests to thrive unchecked. Take your time during application, turning over leaves and inspecting hidden crevices where pests might lurk. Reapplication is also necessary after rain or watering, as both can wash away protective layers. This might seem like extra work, but think of it as an opportunity to reconnect with your garden regularly. Each visit allows you to witness subtle changes and appreciate the resilience of your plants.

Remember, patience is key when using natural pest control methods. They may not offer instant results like chemical alternatives, but their long-term benefits far outweigh any initial delay. By opting for eco-friendly solutions, you're fostering a healthier garden environment and contributing to broader ecological health. As you continue cultivating your container garden, embrace these natural methods as an integral part of your gardening toolkit. They empower you to manage pests effectively while keeping your garden—and the planet—thriving.

As you explore these natural solutions further, consider documenting your experiences in a gardening journal. Note which methods work best for particular pests and how your plants respond over time. This reflection not only enhances your gardening knowledge but also creates a valuable resource for future reference.

PREVENTING AND TREATING FUNGAL DISEASES

Alright, let's delve into the intriguing yet somewhat vexing world of fungal diseases, the uninvited antagonists of the garden drama. These surreptitious adversaries have a knack for appearing when you're least prepared, crafting quite the mess as they spread their touch of mischief. Take powdery mildew, for instance—if you encounter a ghostly white, powdery substance enshrouding your leaves, it's the signature of powdery mildew. It's reminiscent of a careless dusting of flour across your precious foliage. Annoying, isn't it? Meanwhile, lurking beneath the surface is root rot, a stealthy menace that often slips beneath the radar until one day you find your plants drooping forlornly or, in worse scenarios, succumbing to demise. This typically ensues when roots languish in soil that's too saturated, leading to a slow, insidious decay.

To combat the threat of fungi in your garden, adopting smart strategies is essential. Start with considering the importance of air circulation, which is as vital for plants as it is for us. Overcrowded plants struggle to breathe, creating an ideal breeding ground for fungi. Ensure your plants have enough space by pruning them and spacing them properly to improve airflow. Next, assess your watering technique. Overhead watering may seem harmless, but it can leave leaves wet, inviting fungi to take hold. Instead, water the base of the plant, focusing on the roots where water is most needed. This keeps the leaves dry and helps deter fungal diseases.

However, apprehension can set in if fungi decide to pitch camp anyway. Stay calm; solutions abound. For powdery mildew—ever thought a simple kitchen staple like baking soda could be your savior? Mix one tablespoon of baking soda with a gallon of water, enhancing it with a few drops of liquid soap. Douse this mixture on the forlorn leaves witnessing the grim mildew, and prepare to observe its retreat. The magic lies in how baking soda modifies the pH balance on the leaf surfaces, crafting an inhospitable territory for further mildew invasion. On the other hand, when root rot rears its head, it's time for a garden surgery of sorts—a gentle uprooting and transplant operation. Delicately extract the plant from the soil confines, trim away the afflicted root portions, and repot it into fresh, well-draining soil. It's essentially a rejuvenation of your plant's foundational sustenance system.

Moreover, upholding a pristine garden ambiance is a formidable shield against the rampage of fungal diseases. Fallen leaves and debris aren't just untidy; they are potential hotbeds for spores, setting the stage for future infestations. Regularly purging these organic cast-offs can prevent fungi from securing an established foothold. Not to forget, sanitizing your gardening tools between uses is integral, particularly when dealing with contaminated plants. Tools can become unwitting couriers, ferrying spores and exacerbating the spread. A simple concoction of dish soap and water can transform your tools from accomplices back to allies.

Gardening is fundamentally a delicate balance, honed by minute attentions to detail. Fungal diseases may seem daunting upon initial acquaintance, yet through astute preventative measures and timely interventions, you can maintain a firm grip on their spread. Stay observant over the verdant lives you nurture, act swiftly when alterations are detected, and never hesitate to implement corrective measures. Every spot of powdery mildew or lamenting leaf presents itself as an invaluable learning curve, enabling the refinement of your enduring horticultural expertise.

REFLECTION SECTION: YOUR FUNGAL BATTLE PLAN

Take a moment for introspection. Secure a notebook or journal and pen down reflections regarding any fungal ailments you've confronted within your garden realm. Document the victims—specific plants impacted—and recount the strategies you adopted as a counter. Did the baking soda remedy find its application, or did you reassess your watering habits to accommodate the exigencies of plant health? Engaging in such reflective practice fosters a nuanced understanding and bolsters your growing confidence in grappling with fungal adversities.

Stay teeming with vigilance and anticipation, and recognize that tackling fungi is yet another integral chapter in the broader narrative of your gardening journey. Each defensive move and curative action reinforces your bond with the garden oasis you cultivate while solidifying your unwavering commitment as its guardian.

BENEFICIAL INSECTS: NATURE'S PEST CONTROL

In the vibrant and intricate world of container gardening, not all insects are adversaries. Imagine, if you will, a lively army of colorful ladybugs gracefully weaving through your plants, diligently devouring aphids and mites, much like a natural pest control brigade. These sprightly red warriors are more than just a visually delightful spectacle—they are a gardener's steadfast allies, capable of consuming hundreds upon hundreds of aphids throughout their busy lifetimes, boldly patrolling their domain. It's akin to having a specialized, devoted army perpetually on standby, poised and ready to defend your verdant sanctuary from those pesky intruders.

Pass to the valiant parasitic wasp, a tiny, often underrated hero of the garden. These minute warriors lay their inconspicuous eggs inside caterpillars and other garden pests, skillfully regulating their populations in a way that might, on the surface, seem somewhat macabre. However, this natural cycle cleverly sustains the delicate balance in your garden without the slightest reliance on chemical solutions. It's a marvelously efficient process that might seem gruesome but truly exemplifies nature's way of maintaining equilibrium and ensuring only the healthiest of ecosystems flourish.

CRAFTING AN ENTICING ENVIRONMENT

Attracting these benevolent insects transcends mere pest control; it embodies the creation of a thriving ecosystem in the very heart of your garden. These insects offer a sustainable method for managing pests, significantly reducing the need for synthetic chemicals that could damage both your plants and the broader environment. Consider a garden where diversity blossoms, each insect performing its individual role to uphold harmony within the ecosystem. Beneficial insects inherently support this balance by naturally curbing pest populations, thereby empowering your plants to grow more robustly and healthily. Moreover, their mere presence inspires other life forms to flourish, notably enriching your garden's biodiversity.

Envision your garden thriving with life, where each bug plays an integral role. To welcome these helpful creatures, certain adjustments can be effortlessly made. Planting nectar-rich flowers such as the humble alyssum acts as a natural draw for ladybugs and other beneficial insects. These blooms provide much-needed sustenance, enticing these insects to linger. Constructing insect hotels with simple structures filled with natural materials like twigs and bamboo can offer inviting shelters for beneficial bugs. Such cozy retreats allow bugs a tranquil sanctuary to lay eggs and weather any storms. By creating an abundance of food and shelter, you fashion an environment where beneficial insects readily flourish, offering continuous protection against pests.

CONCERNS AND BALANCES

Admittedly, you might worry about enticing too many bugs or upsetting the delicate balance within your garden. But rest assured, nature boasts an astounding talent for self-regulation. Inviting beneficial insects helps manage pest populations without letting any single species claim dominance. Should you notice an abundance of one insect type, observe your garden's dynamics closely. Often, multiple species naturally equilibrate populations over time. Be vigilant for signs of wholesome insect activity—look for ladybugs enjoying aphid meals or wasps busily flitting about their caterpillar hosts.

Addressing concerns about incorporating these creatures into your garden is surprisingly simple. Ensuring balance requires regular garden monitoring and only stepping in when absolutely necessary. If you discover that beneficial insects are thin on the ground, determine if they have ample resources—namely, food, water, and shelter—to thrive. Sometimes, modest alterations like increasing flowering plant varieties or minimizing pesticide usage can make a world of difference. Attentively observing your garden for prolonged periods fosters an understanding of its unique ecosystem and enlightens you on the optimum ways to support it.

EMBRACING THE UNSEEN GUARDIANS

Cultivating an environment that welcomes beneficial insects extends beyond mere plant protection; you are nurturing a miniature ecosystem that thrives on balance and diversity. These minuscule helpers toil tirelessly behind the scenes, ensuring your container garden retains its vitality and resilience. Embrace their formidable yet understated presence as a critical facet of your gardening odyssey—a fundamental element in crafting a vibrant and sustainable outdoor space.

The endeavor of gardening embraces the unexpected, finding splendor in nature's intricate tapestry of life. As you cultivate your container garden, cherish the knowledge that every ladybug and parasitic wasp is a steadfast ally in your mission to maintain a flourishing, pest-free haven. Their presence speaks to nature's remarkable capacity for balance and rejuvenation—a poignant reminder that oftentimes, the smallest creatures yield the most profound impacts on our gardens' health and well-being.

DIY REMEDIES FOR PESTS: RECIPES AND TECHNIQUES

Imagine stepping into your garden, feeling the warmth of the sun on your face, only to be confronted by an army of pests nibbling away at your hard work. Before you reach for commercial chemical sprays, consider some homemade remedies that are both effective and environmentally friendly. Garlic and chili spray is a powerful deterrent against aphids, those pesky little sap-suckers. To make this, blend two cloves of garlic with a few spicy chilis in a quart of water. Let it sit overnight, then strain into a spray bottle. The potent aroma of garlic and the fiery kick from chilis create an unappealing environment for aphids, sending them scurrying away.

Another tried-and-true method is a classic soap and water mixture. Perfect for dealing with soft-bodied insects, this remedy involves mixing one tablespoon of liquid dish soap with a quart of water. The soap disrupts the cell membranes of insects like spider mites, causing them to dehydrate and ultimately perish. Applying this solution with a spray bottle allows you to target specific problem areas without harming beneficial insects. These simple concoctions are easy to whip up with ingredients you likely have at home, making them a convenient first line of defense against garden invaders.

While DIY remedies can be a gardener's best friend, they aren't without their limitations. They work wonders for small-scale infestations but might struggle against more substantial pest populations. Frequent reapplication is often necessary, especially after rain or watering, as these natural solutions can easily wash away. Think of them as part of your regular garden maintenance routine rather than a one-time fix. Although they may require a bit more effort than commercial alternatives, the peace of mind knowing you're not introducing harsh chemicals into your garden is well worth it.

When applying these remedies, safety and plant health should be top priorities. Conduct a spot test on a few leaves before proceeding with full application, as some plants might be more sensitive to certain mixtures. This small step can prevent accidental leaf burn or other damage. Apply these solutions during cooler parts of the day—early morning or late afternoon—when evaporation rates are lower and plant stress is minimized. This careful timing ensures that your plants receive the full benefit of the treatment without unwanted side effects.

Experimentation and adaptation are key to mastering DIY pest control. Feel free to adjust concentrations based on your plants' sensitivity or combine remedies with other natural methods to boost effectiveness. For instance, adding a bit of vegetable oil to your garlic and chili spray can help the mixture adhere better to leaves, increasing its longevity. Keep in mind that each garden is unique, so what works for one might not work for another. Embrace this as an opportunity to learn more about your plants and tailor your approach to their specific needs.

If you're feeling adventurous, consider keeping a garden journal to track your experiments with different remedies. Document what works, what doesn't, and any tweaks you make along the way. This not only helps refine your pest control strategies but also provides valuable insights into your plants' responses over time. Your journal becomes an evolving resource—a personal guide that grows with each season and experience.

Incorporating DIY pest control methods into your gardening routine fosters a sense of empowerment and creativity. You're not just combating pests; you're engaging with your garden on a deeper level, learning its secrets and rhythms. Each recipe you try adds another layer to your understanding of the delicate balance between plants and their environment. With every successful application, you gain confidence in your ability to protect your garden naturally.

So go ahead—experiment, adapt, and discover what works best for your container garden. Embrace these DIY remedies as part of your gardening toolkit, knowing that you're contributing to a healthier garden and a healthier planet. With patience and persistence, you'll find yourself not only nurturing plants but also cultivating your skills and knowledge as a gardener.

CREATING A HEALTHY ECOSYSTEM: PROMOTING PLANT RESILIENCE

In the captivating interplay of nature, a balanced ecosystem assumes the starring role, much like the conductor of a symphony orchestrating harmonious notes. Picture your garden as a self-contained microcosm, a vibrant mini-universe where every leaf, insect, and water droplet plays a crucial part in nurturing a sustainable environment. This delicate web of interconnectedness is essential for naturally minimizing pest and disease pressures, allowing gardeners to reduce reliance on harsh, chemical interventions. By welcoming biodiversity into your garden, you encourage a multitude of life forms that coexist in balance, each contributing uniquely to the overall harmony. Envision incorporating a diverse mix of plants—from exquisite flowering species to lush leafy greens—crafting a kaleidoscopic tapestry that baffles pest populations and fortifies the ecosystem's resilience.

Maintaining soil health stands as another pivotal pillar of a resilient garden. A well-nurtured soil brims with beneficial organisms that enable plants to efficiently fend off diseases while absorbing nutrients. Adopting organic practices, such as composting and mulching, enriches the earth, transforming it into a bountiful banquet of nutrients for your plants. When your soil flourishes, your plants grow more robust and resilient, well-prepared to withstand the caprices of nature. Imagine the transformation as your plants flourish with vigor, drawing strength from the rich, living soil beneath them, intertwining roots with an intricate network of microscopic allies.

To bolster resilience against pests and diseases, initiate by meticulously selecting plant varieties renowned for their resistance. Many seed catalogs proudly showcase these traits, simplifying the process of making informed selections. Additionally, providing balanced nutrition through strategic fertilization holds equal importance. Like humans, plants thrive on a comprehensive and balanced diet. Utilizing slow-release fertilizers ensures they receive a steady influx of essential nutrients over time, reinforcing their natural defenses and improving their robustness. Imagine how, with each passing day, your plants become fortified warriors, equipped to repel potential threats.

Companion planting emerges as another hidden gem in your gardening toolkit. Through strategic pairing of plants, you can significantly enhance overall garden health while naturally deterring pests. Aromatic herbs such as basil and mint can cloak the scent of more vulnerable plants, effectively keeping pests at bay. Alternatively, employing trap crops such as nasturtiums can be a strategic addition to your container garden. These plants serve as sacrificial lures, attracting pests away from your valuable crops. By diverting the attention of insects, nasturtiums effectively safeguard your cherished plants, acting as a natural barrier against unwanted guests. This method not only reduces the need for chemical pesticides but also adds an aesthetic appeal to your gardening space with nasturtiums' vibrant flowers. This shrewd utilization of plant partnerships not only amplifies your garden's productivity but also markedly reduces dependency on chemical interventions. Visualize the bustling life in your garden, where symbiotic plant alliances quietly wage battles against invaders, fostering an organic, thriving ecosystem.

Engaging in regular observation and adaptation plays a critical role in sustaining a balanced ecosystem. Maintaining a garden journal allows you to chronicle changes, detail successful strategies, and document interventions. This valuable practice aids in maintaining a strong connection with your garden's needs, allowing you to decipher patterns over time. By attuning yourself to the seasonal shifts and plant responses, you can fine-tune your practices, ensuring your garden remains a verdant and lively tapestry throughout the year. Imagine yourself as a seasoned detective, piecing together clues in your garden journal, always ready to adapt and refine your strategies.

In conclusion, crafting a robust ecosystem within your container garden hinges on embracing biodiversity, nurturing soil health, selecting resistant plant varieties, and employing strategic companion planting. By cultivating such an environment, you foster a realm where plants flourish naturally with minimal intervention. Continuous observation and adaptation ensure you remain in sync with your garden's dynamic needs, promoting resilience against pests and diseases.

As we draw this chapter on confronting pests and diseases to a close, remember that every challenge presents an opportunity for growth and learning as a gardener. Your garden, like an artist's canvas, is an evolving masterpiece, constantly presenting unexpected discoveries.

CHAPTER 6
ADAPTING TO CLIMATE CHALLENGES

UNDERSTANDING YOUR CLIMATE: MICROCLIMATES AND PLANT HARDINESS

Imagine you're planning a picnic. You check the weather, pack accordingly, and hope for the best. Gardening is somewhat similar, but instead of a weather app, you have the fascinating concept of microclimates right in your backyard. Think of your garden as a patchwork quilt, where each square has its own unique climate. Maybe one corner is sunnier because it's next to a south-facing wall that soaks up heat, while another spot stays cooler in the shade of a tree. Recognizing these variations is key to selecting the right plants for each area.

Microclimates are tiny climate zones within your garden, and they can make a big difference in how your plants grow. A south-facing wall can create a warmer microclimate, perfect for heat-loving plants like peppers or tomatoes. These walls absorb sunlight during the day and release warmth at night, extending the growing season slightly and offering protection during cooler nights. In contrast, shaded areas under trees or beside buildings maintain cooler temperatures, which is ideal for plants that prefer less intense sunlight, like ferns or hostas. Understanding these nuances helps you tailor plant choices to each unique spot.

To truly master your garden's potential, knowing your plant hardiness zone is essential. The USDA Plant Hardiness Zone Map is a fantastic tool for this (https://phzm-prod.ars.usda.gov). It divides regions based on average minimum winter temperatures, helping you determine which plants can survive the winter in your area. But here's the twist: microclimates can exist within these zones, adding another layer of complexity. For example, if your home is in Zone 7 but you have a particularly sheltered spot, it might behave more like Zone 8. Recognizing these differences allows you to push boundaries and experiment with plants that might not typically thrive in your broader zone.

Once you've identified your local hardiness zone and microclimates, adapting your plant choices becomes an exciting game of strategy. In cooler, shaded spots, opt for shade-tolerant plants like lettuce or spinach that appreciate the respite from direct sunlight. These plants thrive without too much heat and can offer lush greenery even in the most tucked-away corners. On the other hand, sunny exposures call for heat-tolerant varieties such as rosemary or lavender, which bask happily in bright light and warm temperatures. By aligning plant preferences with their ideal microclimates, you can create a diverse garden that flourishes across all its varied sections.

To better understand and manage these microclimates, investing in a few simple tools can be invaluable. A basic thermometer helps track temperature variations throughout the day, revealing which areas stay consistently warmer or cooler. Humidity sensors provide insight into moisture levels, helping you adjust watering practices to suit each microenvironment's needs. These tools help you make informed decisions, ensuring each plant receives optimal care tailored to its specific conditions.

INTERACTIVE ELEMENT: CLIMATE MAPPING EXERCISE

Grab a notebook or start a digital journal and map out your garden's microclimates. Spend a week observing how sunlight moves across your space at different times of day. Note temperature fluctuations using a thermometer and identify any particularly dry or damp areas with a humidity sensor. Sketch these observations on paper or digitally to create a microclimate map of your garden. This exercise not only enhances your understanding but also informs future planting decisions by highlighting the diverse conditions within your garden.

Adapting to climate challenges involves more than just choosing the right plants—it's about embracing the dynamic nature of your garden's environment. By recognizing microclimates and understanding plant hardiness zones, you gain the confidence to make informed choices and create a thriving container garden that reflects both nature's diversity and your personal style.

PROTECTING YOUR PLANTS FROM EXTREME WEATHER: HEAT AND FROST

Picture a sweltering summer afternoon, and the gardens are wearing a shimmering, mirage-like haze under the relentless sun. The leaves droop tiredly, silently pleading for respite. It's time to intervene and grant your beloved flora some relief. An innovative and effective way to shield these plants from the scorching sun is by employing shade cloths. These lightweight fabrics act as saviors, gently filtering the sunlight that reaches your garden, subtly reducing the intensity and significantly keeping your precious plants cooler. Imagine draping them artfully over the garden during the peak heat hours of the day, establishing a protective sanctuary bathed in dappled light—a refuge from the merciless rays. This clever yet straightforward method helps prevent unsightly sunburn on leaves that could lead to more severe dehydration, thus lowering the risk of heat stress that might otherwise pummel your garden into wilted submission.

Furthermore, considering the tactile intimacy of mulching—a practice as old as gardening itself—imagine spreading a generous layer of organic mulch, such as straw, shredded bark, or compost around your plantings. This not only serves as a gentle covering but also as a natural temperature moderator. The mulch acts like an insulating blanket, preserving essential moisture within the earth's crust, making sure the soil temperature remains delightfully consistent despite varying atmospheric conditions. With these multifaceted strategies proactively in place, you're essentially fortifying your garden against the arduous summer heat without breaking a sweat, allowing you to enjoy the scene of life sprouting with vigor.

Fast forward to a chilly autumn night when you can envision frost stealthily creeping like a whisper, nipping at the delicate edges of leaves. Frost is indeed treacherous, often appearing out of nowhere and causing significant damage if you're caught unprepared. To combat its stealthy attacks, covering plants with frost blankets or cloches becomes an astoundingly effective defense mechanism. These covers are designed to trap the warmth emitted from the soil, thus encapsulating a cozy microclimate around your plants. Securing the edges is crucial to prevent any sneaky cold air from crawling underneath. For those plants kept in smaller containers, consider relocating them indoors or placing them in sheltered areas like a garage or an enclosed porch. Such a nimble relocation shields the more delicate plants from frost's icy clutches, therefore lending them a fighting chance to breathe life anew when the morning sun returns.

Indeed, sudden weather changes can occasionally catch even the most seasoned gardener off guard, with unpredictable temperature shifts posing a frequent threat. When confronted with such unexpected situations, having a calculated contingency plan is key.

Gardener foresight is invaluable, especially when garden screens or temporary barriers can act as vigilant windbreaks, protecting the plants from chilling gusts that mercilessly strip away accumulated warmth. Should temperatures plummet mysteriously overnight, a simple and effective trick is to water your plants in the evening. This subterfuge works because water naturally retains warmth, slightly elevating soil temperatures through the cold night and providing a semblance of warmth to sustain your plants.

Choosing climate-resilient plants is yet another brilliant way to strengthen your gardening tapestry against weather extremes. In blistering hot climates, consider incorporating heat-tolerant succulents like agave or aloe vera. These resilient beauties thrive with minimal water, happily basking in intense sunlight, rendering them perfect incumbents for sun-drenched locales. Conversely, if you reside in regions tainted by frost, selecting frost-hardy perennials, such as hellebores or Siberian iris, becomes imperative. These valorous plants can withstand cold incursions without wilting, bringing color and vibrancy even when the thermometer's mercury sinks.

Embracing climate-resilient gardening extends beyond mere plant selection; it embodies the nurturing of a resourceful, adaptable mindset to expertly navigate nature's unpredictable whims. As your green thumb gains experience and confidence, you'll soon learn to anticipate local weather patterns, adeptly responding to ever-changing conditions. In time, your garden will not only chirp as a testament to your toil and care but also reflect the resilient spirit of sheer adaptability amid nature's myriad challenges.

By incorporating these diverse strategies and choosing robust plant varieties, you will arm yourself with an arsenal of defenses to protect your garden from both the fierce summer heat and the biting winter frost. Your verdant oasis will thrive through seasonal shifts, offering perennial beauty and bountiful produce, notwithstanding nature's unpredictable temperament.

ADAPTING TO SEASONAL CHANGES: TIPS FOR YEAR-ROUND GARDENING

Think of your garden as a dynamic stage where plants become the protagonists of a fluctuating, ever-evolving performance, responding harmoniously to the seasonal symphony orchestrated by nature. By engaging in the practice of crop rotation, you invigorate this stage, ensuring it remains lively, fertile, and highly productive throughout the year. In the budding days of early spring, cool-season crops such as crisp lettuce, tender spinach, and sweet peas make their grand entrance. These resilient plants enthusiastically embrace the gentle chill of early growth, flourishing vibrantly before the summer sun intensifies its warmth. As the mercury rises, usher in the vibrant cast of warm-season vegetables, including juicy tomatoes, fiery peppers, and crunchy cucumbers. These sun-worshipping stars bask in the swelling heat, offering generous harvests amidst the sultry, sun-drenched months. The art of rotating plants not only enhances your garden's productivity but also plays a crucial role in mitigating soil nutrient depletion, effectively disrupting pest cycles, and encouraging a balanced ecosystem teeming with vibrant life.

Maintaining a garden that enchants year-round demands a touch of foresight paired with a pinch of artistic savvy. By thoughtfully incorporating evergreen foliage, you ensure a perpetual splash of color even during the bleakest days of winter. Stalwarts like boxwood or juniper stand guard, maintaining the vibrancy of your garden landscape as other plants retire from their seasonal duties. Concurrently, planting seasonal annuals such as cheerful pansies in the lively springtime or bright zinnias during the sunlit summer months ensures a steady influx of fresh blooms, continually refreshing your garden's dynamic palette. Selecting plants with varied blooming timelines injects a continuous rhythm of vibrancy and variety, seamlessly transitioning from one season's charm to the next. This curated approach ensures each season brings its own unique flair, transforming your garden into a perpetually appealing visual feast, adorned with colors and resplendent with life.

Extending the growing season stands as a cherished dream for gardeners, a pursuit achievable through the application of clever techniques and inventive solutions. Cold frames function as ingenious miniature greenhouses, artfully capturing sunlight and retaining heat, providing protection to early spring crops from the chilling grasp of frosty nights. Envision these structures as snug sanctuaries where your plants can continue to thrive, defying the brisk air that characterizes early spring. In a similar vein, row covers operate like comforting blankets, gently draped over your garden beds, extending the bounty of the fall harvest by safeguarding plants from cold wind gusts and light frost. Employing these valuable tools allows you to transcend the boundaries traditionally defined by growing seasons, granting you the pleasure of extending your enjoyment of homegrown produce for many months more.

INSIGHTFUL APPROACHES TO SEASONAL PLANNING

Seasonal planning emerges as an indispensable component of any successful gardening endeavor, necessitating the crafting of dedicated task lists tailored to each climate phase, thus elevating the organization and efficiency of your gardening chores. In the rebirth of spring, devotion is set upon preparing the rejuvenating soil and planting the hearty cool-weather crops. Summer ascends with tasks such as vigilantly weeding and adjusting the intricate irrigation systems to accommodate scorching days, thus maintaining steady hydrating love to counter intense evaporation. As fall approaches, it ushers in a period of reflection and preparation. It's a time to tidy up diligently, engaging in thoughtful end-of-season pruning and applying protective mulch to shield dormant plants through the icy grip of winter. Adjustments in watering and nourishing schedules are essential, synchronizing with the shifting seasons to ensure that each plant receives precisely the care it demands at any given time. For instance, during the towering temperatures and intense heat of summer, plants may require more frequent watering regimens or additional nutrients to bolster their rates of growth.

Gardening is a lively and interactive dance with the inexorable cycles of nature, where every season unveils novel opportunities for introspection, learning, and adaptation. Embracing these transformations with open-hearted innovation and understanding sustains your garden's vigor and vibrancy throughout the year. By adeptly rotating crops, selecting plant varieties that maintain perpetual interest, extending growing seasons thoughtfully, and planning activities around seasonal rhythms, you cultivate a resilient garden that thrives, robustly weathering every climatic shift.

The essence of gardening success resides in an attuned awareness of and synchrony with the natural world's rhythms, remaining poised and adaptable amidst nature's dynamic variations. It involves far more than merely sowing seeds; it's about nurturing an interlocking ecosystem that supports and sustains abundant life throughout the entire cyclical journey of the year. By meticulously planning ahead, coupled with doses of creativity and intuitive insight, your container garden blossoms into a perennial source of joy, beauty, and abundant harvest, transcending every seasonal boundary.

CONTAINER GARDENING IN ARID CLIMATES: XERISCAPING AND MORE

Step into a garden bathed in sunlight, a place where every plant tells a story of resilience and smart gardening. This vision captures the spirit of xeriscaping, a gardening philosophy that excels in dry, challenging climates by prioritizing water conservation. In areas where water is a scarce resource, xeriscaping offers a practical guide to crafting stunning, low-maintenance gardens that use water sparingly. The approach centers around choosing drought-resistant plants, the true heroes that withstand intense heat with minimal water. Imagine integrating succulents like jade plants or cacti into your container garden. Their thick, water-storing leaves make them ideal for thriving in hot conditions with little upkeep, embodying the essence of water-efficient gardening.

However, xeriscaping encompasses much more than just the strategic selection of plants; it embodies an artful approach to planting that reduces water use while magnificently maximizing aesthetic appeal. In a container garden, this translates into grouping plants with similar water needs together, ensuring efficient watering practices and minimizing waste. Imagine a thoughtfully arranged cluster of ornamental grasses and native perennials like lavender or yarrow. These plants not only thrive with minimal watering but also add rich texture and vibrant color to your garden palette. By thoroughly understanding the specific water requirements of each plant and positioning them accordingly, you craft a harmonious oasis that requires less from you but invites more from nature's bounty.

Choosing the appropriate soil and containers in arid climates can significantly amplify the success and sustainability of your xeriscaped garden. Terracotta pots, with their naturally porous nature, allow for natural moisture retention while crucially providing the essential airflow needed by plant roots. These timelessly crafted containers not only lend a rustic charm but also effectively support the overarching goal of reducing water loss through evaporation. Pair these pots with water-retentive soil amendments such as vermiculite or coconut coir, which are instrumental in maintaining optimal moisture levels. These materials form the backbone of an environment where plants can truly thrive even in dry conditions. By wisely investing in the right soil and containers, you lay the groundwork for a flourishing garden that admirably defies the often overwhelming challenges posed by an arid climate.

Watering in arid climates requires a degree of finesse and careful thoughtfulness. A drip irrigation system can become your best ally, delivering water directly to the plant roots where it's needed most, thereby minimizing waste and ensuring each precious drop is efficiently utilized. Furthermore, adopting a practice of deep but infrequent watering encourages roots to grow deeper into the soil, seeking out moisture reserves hidden below the surface. Think of it as teaching your plants to become self-sufficient explorers, venturing far and wide in search of sustenance. This approach not only conserves water but also builds resilience in your plants, preparing them to withstand the harshest conditions.

When considering plant selection, cacti and succulents naturally top the list for their minimal water needs and evocatively striking appearances. Imagine a stunning collection of echeverias with their perfectly sculpted rosette forms or a stately row of agaves standing tall and proud. These plants embody the true spirit of xeriscaping, thriving with minimal care while showcasing nature's unparalleled artistry. Beyond these classic options, consider incorporating native plants that are deftly adapted to your local conditions. Over time, they've evolved to withstand the specific challenges of your climate, making them reliable and invaluable additions to any arid garden. Picture wildflowers like California poppies or desert marigolds adding extraordinary splashes of color and texture to your landscape.

Creating a successful container garden in an arid climate is both an artful endeavor and a scientific pursuit. It involves a profound understanding of the unique challenges posed by water scarcity and employing innovative strategies that align harmoniously with nature's rhythms. By fully embracing xeriscaping principles, you invite sustainability into your garden, crafting a space that flourishes magnificently against the odds. From meticulously selecting drought-tolerant plants to expertly choosing the right soil and containers, every decision contributes to a thriving oasis that celebrates resilience, beauty, and creativity. With thoughtful planning and a touch of creativity, your container garden can become a vibrant testament to what's possible even in the harshest environments, dazzling the senses and nurturing the soul.

COPING WITH HUMIDITY: PLANT CHOICES AND CARE STRATEGIES

Gardening in humid climates presents its own unique set of challenges, akin to navigating a thick, damp fog. High humidity can create a breeding ground for fungal diseases, turning your once-thriving garden into a haven for mold and mildew. Imagine the frustration of discovering powdery mildew creeping over your beloved plants, or the disappointment of seeing leaves yellow and wilt under the weight of excess moisture. Managing water levels becomes a delicate balancing act, as too much moisture leads to root rot, while too little can leave your plants parched. The humidity blankets everything, making it tough to maintain the ideal conditions for your green companions.

To combat these challenges, selecting humidity-tolerant plants can make a world of difference. Tropical plants like ferns and orchids thrive in humid environments, their lush foliage and exotic blooms adding a touch of paradise to your garden. These plants have adapted to high humidity, drawing moisture from the air to stay vibrant and healthy. Similarly, vegetables such as okra and peppers perform admirably in these conditions. They relish the warm, moist air and produce bountiful yields when given the care and attention they need. By choosing plants that naturally flourish in humidity, you set your garden up for success.

Managing moisture levels in a humid climate requires a few clever strategies. Increasing air circulation with fans is a simple yet effective way to keep air moving around your plants, reducing the risk of fungal growth. A gentle breeze can do wonders for keeping leaves dry and preventing mold from taking hold. Additionally, using well-draining potting mixes is crucial to prevent water from lingering too long around your plant's roots. These mixes typically contain materials like perlite or sand to facilitate drainage, ensuring that excess water escapes quickly and efficiently.

Humidity often invites unwanted guests—pests that thrive in damp environments. Regular inspection of your plants becomes essential, as early detection can prevent a minor issue from snowballing into a full-blown infestation. Keep an eye out for signs of mold or mildew on leaves and stems, as these can indicate both fungal problems and potential pest activity. Implement preventative pest control measures by maintaining cleanliness in your garden space. Clear away fallen leaves and debris that may harbor pests or diseases, and consider using natural remedies like neem oil or insecticidal soap to deter invaders.

It's also worth noting that some pests, like aphids, are particularly fond of humid conditions. These tiny insects suck sap from plants, weakening them over time. To combat this, ensure your plants are well-nourished and healthy, as robust plants are less likely to fall victim to pest pressures. Consider introducing beneficial insects like ladybugs or lacewings to your garden; they naturally prey on aphids and other common pests, keeping populations in check without the need for harsh chemicals.

For gardeners dealing with relentless humidity, finding harmony between moisture and plant health is key. Experiment with plant placement, ensuring good airflow between containers and within the garden space itself. This simple adjustment can reduce humidity-related issues significantly. Embrace trial and error as you navigate the complexities of humid gardening—each lesson learned brings you closer to mastering these unique conditions.

To further aid in managing high humidity, consider incorporating raised containers or vertical gardening techniques. Elevating plants can improve air circulation around them, reducing the chance of fungal infections. These strategies not only tackle humidity but also make efficient use of space, adding vertical interest to your garden layout.

Incorporating reflective surfaces like light-colored gravel or stones around potted plants can also help mitigate humidity effects by reflecting sunlight and heat, thus moderating soil temperatures. This subtle adjustment contributes to a more balanced environment where plants can continue thriving despite the challenges posed by excessive moisture.

Gardening in humid climates may require some extra effort, but with thoughtful plant selection and strategic care practices, it's entirely possible to cultivate a flourishing container garden. Embrace the lushness that humidity can bring while staying vigilant against its challenges, ensuring your garden remains a vibrant oasis amidst the dampness.

WINTERIZING YOUR CONTAINER GARDEN: PREPARING FOR COLD MONTHS

As the curtain of winter unfolds with its chilly embrace, the task of preparing your container garden for the upcoming cold months takes center stage. Picture the process as tucking your beloved plants into a snug, cozy blanket, ensuring their comfort during the long, dormant stretch until the warmth of spring reappears. One particularly effective method of doing this is by insulating pots with materials such as bubble wrap or burlap. This seemingly simple yet profoundly impactful act provides a much-needed buffer against the relentless bite of cold, especially for containers crafted from materials like ceramic or clay, which are prone to cracking under freezing conditions. By carefully wrapping the chosen insulating material around the pot and securing it with twine, you create a snug cocoon that serves to trap warmth, lovingly shielding your plants from the harshness of winter.

Additionally, in nature, we observe many species coming together for warmth, and your plant containers can do the same.

Grouping them will, much like the instinctive huddle of penguins to preserve heat, allow your plants to share warmth and decrease their exposure to frost's icy grip. As temperatures continue to plunge, consider offering a refuge by moving some of your cherished plants indoors. This transition, however, requires a deft touch to ensure a seamless adjustment to their new indoor environment. Begin by gradually acclimating them to indoor conditions. You can bring them inside for short bursts, incrementally expanding that time over a one or two-week period. This gradual exposure assists them in adapting to the variances in light levels and humidity indoors. Ensuring appropriate light exposure is of the utmost importance, so position the plants near bright windows where they can bask in natural sunlight. If this is not feasible, strategically deploy grow lights to complement natural sunlight. Indoor air, particularly when the heating systems hum into action, can be drier, leading to potential stress for the plants. Thus, consider utilizing a humidifier or placing water trays around plants to uphold adequate moisture levels.

In winter's embrace, plants tend to enter a dormancy phase, demanding care routines that diverge from those during the active growth periods. A pivotal task during this stage is the careful reduction of watering frequency. With growth slowing to a gentle halt, the plants inherently require less water, and overwatering can be a slippery slope to root rot. Regularly feeling the soil's moisture status provides a useful guide, watering only when the soil feels dry about an inch beneath the surface. Another essential task is the meticulous pruning of any dead or damaged foliage. This invigoration helps channel the plant's energy towards bolstering its healthy components while simultaneously warding against potential pest infestations.

Winter is not synonymous with neglect; rather, it invites regular checks to ensure your plants maintain their vigor. Keep a vigilant watch on indoor plants, scanning for any signs of pest activity, such as the unwelcome presence of spider mites or aphids. These minute disrupters can stealthily infiltrate indoor sanctuaries and unleash havoc if not promptly addressed. By regularly inspecting leaves and stems, and gently wiping them with a damp cloth if necessary, you can maintain their health and vitality. As fluctuating temperatures weave through the season, remain adaptable with your care routine. If you detect yellowing or falling leaves, it might well signal an opportune moment to tweak your regime of watering or light exposure.

The essence of winterizing your container garden lies in harmonizing with the season's natural rhythms while ensuring your plants are primed to flourish come spring. Through actions such as insulating pots, adjusting indoor light and humidity levels, and meticulously tailoring care routines, you provide the vital support your plants need through their dormant phase.

As we draw this chapter on adapting to climate challenges to a close, remember that gardening is a thriving discourse with nature itself. Every season unfurls unique lessons and opportunities for both your plants and yourself as a gardener to learn and grow. Embrace these changes with an open heart, and you will likely discover joy infused in every phase of your gardening adventure.

CHAPTER 7
SUSTAINABLE AND ECO-FRIENDLY PRACTICES

COMPOSTING FOR CONTAINER GARDENERS: CREATING YOUR OWN FERTILIZER

Picture this: you're working in your kitchen, peeling carrots, and instead of tossing those peels into the trash can—a place where they'd typically contribute to the burgeoning mass of landfill waste—you embark on a transformative journey by turning them into rich, nourishing compost. This simple action revitalizes the very container garden you take such pride in cultivating. Composting transcends mere waste recycling; it is about establishing a sustainable, miniature ecosystem right at your doorstep. By turning what would be kitchen scraps into a valuable resource, you're not only reducing landfill waste but also effectively diminishing the production of methane emissions, which play a significant role as greenhouse gases in climate change. This is a small yet impactful contribution to lessening global environmental challenges. Yet, the process doesn't end with waste reduction. Compost introduces essential organic matter to your soil, improving its structure and augmenting its nutrient content. This transformation results in healthier plants and a more vibrant display of blooms that mark the success of your horticultural efforts.

Starting your composting venture is far less daunting than it may appear, even for those with limited space. A compact compost bin or a sleek tumbler can easily find its home on a balcony or a discreet corner of your yard. To initiate this process, you'll begin by layering green materials such as vegetable scraps and coffee grounds, alongside brown materials like dried leaves and shredded paper. This balance between greens, which are nitrogen providers, and browns, the carbon contributors, is critical for the decomposition process. For novices, aiming for a balanced ratio of 1:2 between greens and browns is advisable for achieving optimal results. The compost pile should maintain a level of moisture akin to a wrung-out sponge—neither too dry nor overly saturated—and it's crucial to aerate it by turning it weekly. This practice accelerates the composting process by introducing vital oxygen, which sustains the microorganisms responsible for decomposition.

An understanding of what can be tossed into your compost pile is just as vital as knowing what to exclude. Vegetable scraps are ideal candidates—imagine a variety of carrot tops, potato peels, and wilted spinach leaves. In addition, coffee grounds, eggshells, and tea bags contribute effectively to the organic mix. However, certain items such as meat and dairy products should be avoided, as they are prone to attracting pests and developing unpleasant odors. Similarly, steer clear of oily foods and anything that has been treated with chemicals, as these can disrupt the compost's natural balance. By adhering to natural materials, you can ensure that your compost remains both nutrient-rich and safe for your beloved plants.

Once your efforts have produced a batch of rich, earthy compost, it's time to apply it within the realm of your container garden. Incorporate the compost into your potting soil to enhance its fertility, thereby providing your plants an advantageous start with accessible nutrients right from the roots. Furthermore, you can deploy the compost as a top dressing by gently sprinkling a thin layer over the soil's surface. This method acts as a slow-release fertilizer, gradually doling out nutrients each time you water your plants, fostering growth without the need for chemical alternatives.

Composting Checklist

- **Setup**: Select an appropriately sized bin or tumbler that suits your space.
- **Layering**: Construct alternating layers of green materials (such as veggie scraps) with brown materials (like dry leaves and shredded paper).
- **Maintenance**: Ensure consistent moisture levels, turning the pile regularly each week to promote aeration.
- **Materials**: Incorporate coffee grounds and other organic materials; avoid including meat, dairy, and other non-compostable items.
- **Usage**: Blend with potting soil for enhanced fertility or apply as a top dressing to nourish plants continually.

Composting transcends traditional eco-friendly practices and emerges as a fulfilling, cyclical process of growth and renewal. By embedding it into your gardening routine, you'll observe that it not only considerably reduces waste but also profoundly enriches the life that blossoms around you. This virtuous cycle turns household leftovers into vibrant blooms and lush greenery within your containers. Each motion of the compost pile isn't merely about fostering plant life, but a continuous, positive contribution to the environment. This collaborative effort between nature and your sustainable gardening becomes a powerful testament to the marvels of nature and your enduring commitment to a greener, more sustainable world. Despite being a modest step on a personal level, it has the power to effect significant differences in cultivating a more eco-conscious world.

UPCYCLING CONTAINERS: CREATIVE AND SUSTAINABLE SOLUTIONS

Imagine transforming your living space with a splash of creativity, breathing new life into items once destined for the landfill. Upcycling is more than just a trend; it's a vibrant expression of sustainability and individuality. By repurposing old materials, you contribute to environmental conservation, reducing waste by giving these forgotten objects a second chance. This practice not only alleviates the pressure on waste management systems but also curtails the demand for new resources, effectively diminishing your carbon footprint. More than just a green initiative, upcycling allows for personal expression, enabling you to craft unique garden aesthetics that reflect your personality. In doing so, you create a garden that stands out, not just for its beauty but also for its commitment to sustainability.

With a bit of imagination, ordinary household items can become extraordinary planters. Consider those old boots gathering dust in your closet. By transforming them into quirky planters, you add character and whimsy to your garden, while also keeping those boots out of the trash. Simply fill them with soil and a plant of your choice, and watch as they become a charming focal point. Similarly, mason jars can find new life as herb gardens on your kitchen windowsill. Their clear glass beautifully showcases the soil layers and root structures, turning a simple jar into an intriguing display. For a rustic touch, hang them with twine or wire to create a suspended herb garden that's both practical and visually appealing.

Before starting any upcycling project, it's important to prepare your materials carefully. This ensures your creations are both functional and durable. When repurposing items like cans or jars, drill small drainage holes at the bottom to prevent water from accumulating and causing root rot. For items made of porous materials, like old wooden crates or terracotta pots, apply a non-toxic sealant inside to prevent leaks and extend their lifespan. These simple steps are crucial for ensuring your plants thrive in their new homes. Not only do they help maintain optimal growing conditions, but they also protect your creations from wear and tear over time.

Upcycling is all about creativity and experimentation. Don't be afraid to mix materials and colors for an eclectic look that's uniquely yours. Combine metal tubs with wooden crates or weave textiles into your designs for added texture and warmth. The possibilities are endless, limited only by your imagination. Share your creations on social media platforms to inspire others and join a community of upcyclers who are passionate about sustainability and innovation. This not only spreads awareness about eco-friendly practices but also connects you with like-minded individuals who share your enthusiasm for creative gardening.

A great way to delve deeper into upcycling is by joining online forums or local workshops dedicated to sustainable gardening practices. These spaces offer a wealth of knowledge and inspiration, helping you refine your skills and discover new ideas. They also provide opportunities to showcase your projects and receive feedback from fellow enthusiasts. As you continue to explore this rewarding practice, remember that upcycling is not just about the end result; it's about the process of transforming something ordinary into something extraordinary. This journey fosters creativity, encourages sustainable living, and ultimately leads to a more personalized and meaningful connection with your garden.

Upcycling is more than a hobby; it's a lifestyle choice that reflects a commitment to sustainability and creativity. It invites you to see potential where others see waste, transforming discarded items into beautiful garden pieces that tell a story. Each upcycled container becomes a testament to innovation and resourcefulness, offering a unique blend of function and art. As you experiment with different materials and designs, you'll find that upcycling enriches not only your garden but also your life, fostering a deeper appreciation for the beauty in repurposing and reinvention.

So why not take a look around your home or neighborhood for items that can be given a second life? Let your imagination run wild as you transform everyday objects into stunning garden features that reflect your commitment to both style and sustainability. In doing so, you'll create spaces that are not only environmentally friendly but also uniquely yours—a reflection of your creativity, values, and passion for gardening in harmony with nature.

WATER-WISE GARDENING: REDUCING YOUR ENVIRONMENTAL IMPACT

Water-wise gardening is all about efficiency. It's about choosing plants that naturally thrive with less water and optimizing how and when you water them. Drought-tolerant plants are your best friends here. Think succulents, lavender, or yarrow. These hardy species have adapted to survive with little moisture. They store water in their leaves or have deep root systems that tap into groundwater. By selecting these resilient plants, you create a garden that can withstand dry spells without constant attention.

Once you've chosen your plants, consider how you will water them. Timing is everything. Watering early in the morning or late in the evening reduces evaporation, ensuring more moisture reaches the roots. It's like giving your plants a refreshing drink just when they need it most. This timing also helps prevent diseases that can thrive on wet foliage left to sit overnight.

Installing a drip irrigation system is another effective strategy. This system delivers water directly to the plant's roots, minimizing waste and maximizing efficiency. It's like having a personal assistant for your garden, making sure each plant gets exactly what it needs without the guesswork. Drip systems are easy to set up and can be adjusted for different plant types, ensuring a customized watering plan.

Capturing rainwater is another excellent way to conserve resources. Installing a rain barrel under your downspout collects free water from the sky, which you can use to hydrate your garden during dry periods. This not only saves on your water bill but also makes use of natural resources that might otherwise be wasted. Rainwater is free from the chemicals found in tap water, making it a healthier option for your plants.

Mulching plays a significant role in water conservation, too. A layer of mulch acts like a protective blanket for your soil. Organic options like straw or leaf litter are ideal, as they gradually decompose and enrich the soil while retaining moisture. Mulching keeps the soil cool and reduces evaporation, ensuring your plants stay hydrated longer. Plus, it suppresses weeds, which would otherwise compete with your plants for precious water.

Different plants benefit from various mulching techniques. For instance, vegetables might do well with straw mulch, which is light and easy to move around as needed. Ornamental plants might enjoy leaf litter or bark mulch for a more aesthetic touch. Experiment with what works best for your garden, keeping in mind the specific needs of each plant species.

Engaging with community initiatives on water conservation can amplify your efforts. Local workshops often provide valuable insights into sustainable gardening practices tailored to your region's climate and resources. Participating in these events not only expands your knowledge but also connects you with fellow gardeners who share your passion for sustainability.

Advocating for sustainable practices within community gardens can inspire broader change. By sharing your success stories with neighbors or collaborating on community projects like setting up rainwater collection systems, you contribute to a collective effort towards environmental responsibility. These actions foster a sense of community and show how individual efforts can lead to significant impacts.

Gardening with a focus on water conservation transforms your space into an environmentally conscious haven. The practices not only support plant health but also align with broader goals of sustainability and resource management. As you implement these strategies, you'll find a deeper connection to your garden and the natural world around you.

Creating a water-wise garden is an ongoing process of learning and adaptation. Each season presents new challenges and opportunities for growth, both for you and your plants. Embrace the journey of discovering what works best in your unique environment, knowing that every small step you take adds up to meaningful change. With each droplet saved, each plant that flourishes under your care, you contribute to a larger narrative of sustainability and stewardship of our planet's precious resources.

Water-wise gardening isn't just about conserving water; it's about cultivating mindfulness and intentionality in how we interact with our environment. It's about recognizing our role in the ecosystem and making choices that reflect our values of stewardship and care for the earth. As we continue to explore sustainable practices in our gardens, we find not only beauty and abundance but also a profound sense of purpose and connection to the natural world.

ORGANIC GARDENING PRACTICES: SAFE AND NATURAL TECHNIQUES

Organic gardening is more than just avoiding synthetic chemicals; it's a commitment to fostering a harmonious relationship with nature. This approach emphasizes biodiversity, building healthy soil, and nurturing plants without resorting to artificial aids. By steering clear of synthetic fertilizers and pesticides, you protect the environment and create a safer space for children and pets. This method promotes a thriving ecosystem right in your backyard or balcony, encouraging beneficial insects and microorganisms to flourish.

Managing pests and diseases organically might seem challenging at first, but nature provides its own solutions. Homemade insecticidal soap sprays are a practical option. You can make these by mixing mild soap with water, which effectively tackles soft-bodied insects like aphids without harming beneficials like ladybugs. Another powerful ally is companion planting. Certain plants deter pests naturally or attract beneficial insects that prey on garden nuisances. For instance, marigolds repel nematodes, while basil keeps mosquitoes at bay. Placing these plants strategically can significantly reduce pest issues, making your garden healthier without the need for chemicals.

Soil health is the backbone of any flourishing garden. Organic amendments like worm castings and rock dust play a pivotal role here. Worm castings are essentially worm manure, packed with nutrients that improve soil fertility and boost plant growth. They're easy to incorporate into your garden routine—just mix them into the top layer of soil or use them as a side dressing around your plants. Another treasure for your soil is rock dust. Rich in trace minerals, it enhances soil structure and helps plants absorb nutrients more efficiently. Regularly adding these amendments ensures your soil remains healthy, supporting robust plant growth.

Sourcing organic seeds and plants is another cornerstone of sustainable gardening. Choosing organic options means they haven't been treated with harmful chemicals, supporting cleaner, safer food production. Heirloom varieties are particularly valuable. These seeds pass down unique traits through generations, helping preserve genetic diversity—a vital component in resilient ecosystems. By planting heirlooms, you're not only growing food but also contributing to biodiversity. Supporting local organic seed suppliers further strengthens community ties and promotes sustainable agriculture.

Switching to organic gardening might seem daunting initially, but it's about making small changes that collectively make a big difference. Start by gradually replacing synthetic products with organic alternatives. Observe how your garden responds and adjust accordingly. You'll soon discover that organic gardening fosters a deeper connection to the natural world, encouraging you to learn from the environment around you.

Embracing organic practices transforms your garden into a vibrant ecosystem where every element plays its part. It's about working with nature rather than against it, creating a balanced environment where plants thrive with minimal intervention. As you cultivate your organic garden, you'll find that this approach not only benefits your plants but also enriches your understanding of the intricate web of life that surrounds us.

Engaging in organic gardening also opens the door to community involvement. Joining local gardening groups or attending workshops can provide valuable insights and support as you navigate this journey. Sharing experiences with fellow gardeners helps build a network of like-minded individuals committed to sustainable practices.

As you explore organic gardening, remember that it's a continuous process of learning and adaptation. Each season presents new challenges and opportunities for growth, both for you and your plants. Embrace these experiences as part of the journey towards creating a healthier, more sustainable garden.

The joy of organic gardening lies in its simplicity and effectiveness. It's about finding creative solutions to challenges and discovering the satisfaction that comes from growing plants naturally. Whether you're cultivating vegetables, herbs, or flowers, organic practices offer a holistic approach that nurtures both your garden and your soul.

Incorporating these techniques into your gardening routine transforms it from a mere hobby into an enriching experience that supports biodiversity and promotes environmental stewardship.

As you continue on this path, you'll discover that organic gardening is not just a method but a way of life—a meaningful connection to the earth and its rhythms.

BUILDING A SUSTAINABLE CONTAINER GARDEN: LONG-TERM TIPS

Creating a sustainable container garden isn't just about what you plant today but how you nurture it over time. One key practice is rotating your crops to prevent soil depletion. Just like in traditional farming, different plants use and replenish various nutrients. By changing what you grow in each pot seasonally, you keep the soil balanced and healthy. Imagine your basil thriving this summer, only to swap places with a lovely array of radishes come fall. This simple rotation helps break cycles of pests and diseases, ensuring a fresh start for each planting season.

Encouraging beneficial insects is another natural way to enhance your garden's health. These tiny allies, like ladybugs and bees, play a crucial role in pollination and pest control. You can attract them by planting flowers like marigolds or lavender along-side your veggies. This biodiversity creates a balanced ecosystem where plants thrive, and harmful pests stay at bay. It's like inviting helpful little friends to your garden party, each bringing something valuable to the table.

Minimizing waste in your garden is not only eco-friendly but also cost-effective. Consider using biodegradable pots for seedlings. They break down naturally in the soil, adding nutrients as they decompose. This eliminates the need for plastic containers and reduces waste. When your plants outgrow their pots, simply plant them directly into larger containers or the ground. Composting plant debris is another excellent way to recycle nutrients back into your garden. Leaves, spent flowers, and pruned branches can all be composted rather than discarded. This reduces waste and enriches the soil, closing the loop on your gardening cycle.

Maintaining garden health requires regular attention and care. Begin with soil testing to understand its nutrient profile, making amendments as needed. Kits are available that make this process straightforward, helping you identify deficiencies before they affect plant health. Adding organic matter like compost improves soil structure and fertility, giving your plants the best possible environment to grow. Pruning and grooming are equally important for plant vitality. Regularly remove dead or diseased leaves and trim overgrown branches to promote airflow and light penetration. This not only keeps plants looking neat but also prevents disease.

Continuous learning is vital in sustainable gardening. New techniques and practices emerge regularly, offering innovative ways to improve your garden's sustainability. Reading books, articles, or blogs keeps you informed about the latest trends and ideas. Attending workshops or online courses provides hands-on experience and connects you with other gardeners who share your passion for sustainability. Engaging with community groups or online forums can also be a great source of inspiration and support, especially when facing challenges.

Experimentation is an integral part of sustainable gardening. Trying out new plants or techniques can lead to exciting discoveries about what works best in your space. Keep a garden journal to track your successes and failures, noting what you learn along the way. This record becomes invaluable over time, providing insights that help refine your approach each season. Sharing your experiences with others fosters a sense of community and encourages collaboration on sustainable gardening projects.

Gardening sustainably in containers is a dynamic process that evolves with each season and every new idea you explore. It's about creating a living space that reflects both your values and creativity while contributing positively to the environment. By implementing these long-term strategies, you cultivate not just plants but a thriving ecosystem that supports biodiversity and resilience.

Every small change you make today lays the groundwork for a healthier garden tomorrow, so don't hesitate to experiment and adapt as you go along.

SUPPORTING LOCAL WILDLIFE: CREATING HABITATS IN SMALL SPACES

Imagine the unyielding joy that fills your spirit as you wander through your garden—the delightful array of colors, the intoxicating aromas, and the lively presence of countless living organisms. Picture adding to this the soft, engaging hum of bees darting from blossom to blossom or the delicate, mesmerizing dance of butterflies flitting around. By nurturing a garden that bolsters local wildlife, you're not merely offering a lifeline to various creatures; you are enriching the whole ecological network that is interconnected with your own charming oasis of green. Pollinators, such as bees and butterflies, are integral in ensuring the flora in your garden efficiently produce their extraordinary blooms and nourishing fruits. Meanwhile, birds, along with beneficial insects, are nature's soldiers, tirelessly working to regulate pest populations, maintaining a natural balance. Hence, a garden teeming with diversity becomes an emblem of health and vibrancy.

Creating an inviting environment for a myriad of wildlife in your smaller garden space need not be a daunting task. The journey can simply begin with the introduction of native flowers, which act as a beckoning call to local pollinators. These plants, with their natural evolution alongside indigenous fauna, provide the perfect nectar and pollen that pollinators have long come to rely upon. Think of it as laying out a sumptuous spread brimming with their all-time favorite delicacies. Plants like coneflowers, black-eyed Susans, and milkweed stand as stellar selections to beckon bees and butterflies. Beyond flora, adding a humble bird feeder or even a simple basin of water can work wonders in drawing avian visitors. These birds become more than just intriguing sights to behold; they are active participants in pest control, consuming insects that would otherwise be detrimental to your delicate plants.

Venturing further into supporting various species, try creating miniaturized habitats within your garden containers. Introducing a small log or strategically scattered stones can serve as sanctuary zones for beneficial insects such as beetles and ladybugs. These industrious creatures play essential roles in breaking down organic materials and naturally managing plant pests. Consider also including a tiny water feature — even a shallow dish filled with fresh water can attract amphibians like frogs or offer a much-needed sip to birds and insects. Each of these elements weaves together a small but profound ecosystem within your garden, nurturing and sustaining life across various levels.

Broader community involvement can significantly amplify your efforts to foster local wildlife. By joining or initiating local wildlife conservation groups, you connect with others who share your passion for preserving nature. Working together on community initiatives such as habitat restoration projects not only bolsters environmental well-being but also creates bonds of friendship and shared purpose among participants. Whether it's planting native species along a scenic local trail or fashioning wildlife-friendly zones in urban areas, every little action contributes to a sizable environmental impact.

When you inspire friends and neighbors to adopt wildlife-inclusive practices, you expand your influence beyond the confines of your own garden. Sharing seeds, offering gardening tips, and exchanging success anecdotes serves to motivate others, collectively forming a network of gardens that enhance biodiversity. Such synergy acts as a ripple, extending positive outcomes far beyond personal efforts, fortifying local ecosystems as more gardens transform into refuges for wildlife.

By aiding wildlife, you embed yourself into the sweeping story of conservation and stewardship. Your garden, while still a personal escape, becomes an essential piece in the larger ecological puzzle, contributing to the fortitude and flourishing of local ecosystems. The vibrant sights and harmonious sounds brought by wildlife infuse an added depth of delight into your gardening pursuits, making it a living testament to the profound and beautiful interconnectedness of nature.

In this chapter, we've unfolded how even compact spaces can yield significant environmental contributions through sustainable endeavors like composting, upcycling, judicious water management, organic gardening, and creating hospitable environments for wildlife. Each tactic not only enriches your surroundings but also uplifts environmental health. As we advance to the next chapter, we'll explore ways to tackle common challenges in container gardening, equipping you with tangible solutions to secure ongoing success with your blooming, eco-friendly garden.

These methodologies do more than just benefit the environment; they metamorphose your gardening routine into a pursuit that's deeply meaningful and impactful. With every sustainable step, you're nurturing the planet, gradually cultivating it into a healthier version of itself, container by container. Embrace these practices wholeheartedly and relish in observing your garden's transformation into a thriving, self-sustaining ecosystem.

CHAPTER 8
TROUBLESHOOTING
AND SUCCESS STORIES

COMMON CONTAINER GARDENING MISTAKES AND HOW TO AVOID THEM

One of the most frequent mistakes is overcrowding. The urge to cram many plants into a single pot can be overwhelming. Initially, it might seem like a good idea, as you imagine a pot brimming with life, with the plants standing tall like a supportive community. However, the reality is that they will compete intensely for the limited nutrients and water available, which ultimately stunts their growth. A better approach is to give each plant the breathing room it deserves. A good rule of thumb is to limit your selection to one or perhaps two plants for larger containers. This ensures that each has enough room to spread its roots and access the resources it needs to thrive beautifully.

Additionally, pitfalls lie in the choice of soil. Garden soil from your backyard may appear handy and cost-effective, but it compacts too easily, which can suffocate roots and prevent adequate drainage. This can be a silent saboteur in your gardening efforts. Instead, opting for container-specific potting mixes is highly recommended. These specialized blends are scientifically formulated to provide the optimal balance of nutrients and aeration needed for container plants. Common ingredients include peat moss or coconut coir, which have natural moisture-retaining qualities without risking the dreaded waterlogging of your plants. Choosing appropriate soil is undeniably crucial for promoting healthy root development and ensuring overall plant vigor.

A little research into each plant's unique needs can make a world of difference. Familiarize yourself with their light, water, and soil preferences before your trowel touches earth. Planning your garden layout thoughtfully can prevent potential problems. Consider how much space each plant will require as it grows, and evaluate how much sunlight your garden area receives throughout the day. By sketching a rough plan before planting, you'll ensure that your garden is not only aesthetically pleasing but also functional and sustainable over time.

The impacts of these initial mistakes can be significant. Overcrowded pots result in reduced yields as plants vie for the limited resources they so desperately need. This competition also makes them more vulnerable to pests and diseases, as stressed plants can attract unwanted visitors looking to exploit their weakened state. Inadequate soil leads to poor drainage, which, in turn, can cause root rot—a stealthy killer in many container gardens. By addressing these concerns proactively, you can save yourself both time and frustration. This preparation fosters a bountiful harvest of healthy, thriving plants, transforming what could have been a disappointing venture into a rewarding and visually spectacular outcome.

INTERACTIVE EXERCISE: PLANNING YOUR PERFECT CONTAINER GARDEN

Take a creative journey by grabbing a notebook or even a whiteboard, and let your imagination run wild by sketching your ideal container garden layout. As you do, note the sunlight exposure for each potential spot, and strategically plan which plants will inhabit each area based on their specific light needs and mature size. Armed with this visual blueprint, be sure to list any questions or uncertainties you may have about the specific requirements of certain plants. To gather the answers, delve into reputable online gardening resources or consult traditional gardening guides. This exercise is more than just a plan; it's a powerful visualization of your garden's eventual potential, and it serves as a guide for making methodical and informed planting choices.

Mistakes are an inevitable part of the gardening learning curve. They're not seen merely as setbacks, but as opportunities to grow your skills and deepen your relationship with the plant world. By gaining an understanding of these common pitfalls and taking proactive steps to mitigate them, you can cultivate a thriving container garden that consistently brings you joy and satisfaction, season after abundant season. Gardener, embrace the process—from the first seed to the last flower—and watch as you develop not only a beautiful garden but also a deeper understanding and appreciation for nature's delicate balance.

DIAGNOSING PLANT PROBLEMS: SYMPTOMS AND SOLUTIONS

Imagine walking out to your container garden, only to notice that the once vibrant leaves of your beloved basil are turning yellow. It's easy to feel a wave of panic, but fear not—this is where a little detective work comes in handy. Yellowing leaves often signal a nutrient deficiency, specifically nitrogen, which is crucial for lush, green foliage. When you see this symptom, consider adding an organic fertilizer rich in nitrogen to rejuvenate your plant's vigor. Wilting, on the other hand, could be a sign of water imbalance. If your plants look droopy despite regular watering, you might be overwatering them. Check the soil moisture; if it feels soggy, it's time to let it dry out a bit before the next watering session.

To effectively troubleshoot plant problems, having a checklist can be your best ally. Start by examining your plants for signs of pests or diseases. Look under leaves and around stems for any unwanted guests like aphids or fungus gnats. Next, test the soil's pH and moisture levels. A simple pH meter can help you determine if the soil is too acidic or alkaline, which can impact nutrient availability. For moisture, stick your finger into the soil about an inch deep—if it feels dry, your plant might need a drink. Alternatively, if it feels too wet, scaling back on watering is wise. Observing these factors can often lead you directly to the root of the issue.

Understanding what causes plant problems is key to prevention and recovery. Poor drainage is a leading cause of root rot, a condition where roots become waterlogged and begin to decay. Ensure your containers have adequate drainage holes and avoid using heavy garden soil that retains too much water. Similarly, insufficient sunlight can stunt plant growth, leaving them spindly and weak. Make sure your sun-loving plants get at least six hours of direct sunlight daily to thrive. If lighting is an issue, consider rearranging your garden to optimize sun exposure or investing in grow lights for indoor setups.

Once you've identified the problem, implementing effective remedies is crucial. Adjust watering schedules based on your plant's specific needs—most prefer consistent moisture but not constant saturation. When nutrient deficiencies are the culprit, incorporate organic fertilizers or soil amendments to replenish missing elements. Products like worm castings or compost can work wonders in providing a balanced nutrient profile. These solutions not only restore health but also strengthen your plants against future stressors.

CONTAINER GARDEN TROUBLESHOOTING CHECKLIST

Symptom	Possible Cause(s)	Steps to Diagnose & Resolve
Yellowing Leaves	- Nitrogen deficiency - Overwatering or poor drainage - Root-bound plant	☑ Check for soggy soil and drainage holes ☑ Test soil nitrogen levels or fertilize with balanced fertilizer ☑ Gently remove plant from pot to check for root crowding
Wilting (even with wet soil)	- Root rot from overwatering - Poor drainage or compacted soil - Fungal disease	☑ Inspect roots for dark, mushy texture (sign of rot) ☑ Improve drainage or repot in fresh, well-aerated mix ☑ Disinfect pot and prune dead roots
Wilting (dry soil)	- Underwatering - Too small a container - Excessive sun or wind	☑ Water deeply and slowly ☑ Upgrade to a larger pot if roots are bound ☑ Provide shade during peak heat
Brown Leaf Tips or Edges	- Salt buildup from fertilizer - Low humidity or underwatering - Pot too hot in direct sun	☑ Flush pot with clean water to remove excess salts ☑ Mist leaves or increase humidity ☑ Place pots on trays or use insulating materials

Symptom	Possible Cause(s)	Steps to Diagnose & Resolve
Stunted Growth	- Nutrient deficiency (e.g., phosphorus or potassium) - Compact soil or rootbound - Low light levels	☑ Fertilize with a complete slow-release or liquid fertilizer ☑ Check for root crowding and loosen or repot ☑ Relocate to a brighter area
Leaf Spots or Blotches	- Fungal or bacterial disease - Pest damage - Sunburn from water droplets	☑ Remove affected leaves ☑ Apply organic fungicide if needed ☑ Water at soil level and avoid leaf splash
Holes or Chewed Leaves	- Aphids, caterpillars, slugs, beetles	☑ Inspect underside of leaves ☑ Spray with insecticidal soap or neem oil ☑ Handpick large pests or set up traps

Symptom	Possible Cause(s)	Steps to Diagnose & Resolve
Powdery or Sticky Residue	- Powdery mildew - Aphids or whiteflies (honeydew)	☑ Use horticultural oil or fungicide for mildew ☑ Wipe leaves, rinse plants, or spray insecticidal soap
Pale or Discolored Leaves	- Iron or magnesium deficiency - Alkaline soil pH	☑ Use a soil pH test kit (target pH ~6.0–6.8) ☑ Apply chelated iron or magnesium as needed ☑ Consider repotting with acidic potting mix if needed
No Flowers or Fruit	- Too much nitrogen - Not enough light - Wrong temperature range	☑ Use low-nitrogen, high-phosphorus fertilizer ☑ Ensure 6–8 hrs of sunlight/day ☑ Protect plants from temperature extremes

TESTING & MONITORING TIPS

- **Soil Moisture:** Use your finger or a moisture meter to check 2" below the surface.

  - **Soil pH:** Use a pH test kit or digital tester; amend with sulfur (to lower) or lime (to raise).

  - **Nutrient Deficiency:** Look for pattern—older vs. younger leaves affected can point to different deficiencies.

  - **Pests:** Inspect both sides of leaves, stems, and soil surface regularly.

Navigating plant problems might seem daunting at first, but with practice and patience, it becomes second nature. Each symptom tells a story about what's happening below the surface, and learning to interpret these signs enhances your gardening prowess. The satisfaction of nursing a struggling plant back to health is immense—it's like solving a mystery with a happy ending. Keep experimenting and observing; every challenge is an opportunity to deepen your understanding of the fascinating world of container gardening.

SUCCESS STORIES: INSPIRING JOURNEYS FROM BEGINNER TO PRO

In the hustle and bustle of city life, a rooftop garden can be a slice of paradise. Take Emma, a city dweller who transformed her cramped balcony into a lush green haven. When she first started, Emma didn't know the difference between a trowel and a spade. Yet, with dedication, she now grows everything from juicy tomatoes to fragrant herbs in her small space. Her secret? Consistent observation and adaptability. She checks her plants daily, adjusting water and sunlight as needed. This hands-on approach allows her to spot issues early and find creative solutions.

Another inspiring tale is of Jake, who sought self-sufficiency through homegrown veggies. Living in an apartment with no yard, he turned to container gardening as a way to produce his own food. With limited space, Jake became innovative. He used vertical gardening techniques to maximize his growing area, hanging pots on walls to save room. His home is now filled with a bounty of produce, from crunchy bell peppers to sweet strawberries. His success lies in his willingness to learn and experiment, trying new methods until he found what worked best.

Challenges are part of every gardener's story. Emma faced climate issues, with her plants wilting under the harsh summer sun. Rather than give up, she researched shade cloths and set up a makeshift shelter to protect her plants. Jake battled pests early on, losing his first batch of basil to hungry aphids. Instead of being discouraged, he explored natural pest control methods like neem oil, which helped him safeguard future crops. These stories illustrate that setbacks are not failures but stepping stones towards success.

Setting achievable goals is key. Start with something small, like growing a single type of herb or flower, and build from there. Celebrate each milestone—your first flower bloom or the first tomato you pick. These small victories build confidence and inspire further growth. Emma plans to expand her garden by adding more flowering plants next season, while Jake has his sights set on trying his hand at container-grown potatoes. Each goal reached fuels the next adventure.

In the world of container gardening, creativity reigns supreme. Emma uses recycled containers and old buckets as planters, finding beauty in repurposing everyday items. Jake shares his space with local wildlife, setting up a small birdbath that attracts pollinators and adds life to his garden. Their stories prove that you don't need a large plot of land to create something extraordinary. With a bit of imagination and resourcefulness, even the smallest space can become a thriving garden.

Remember that every gardener started as a beginner. The path from novice to expert is paved with trial and error, learning from each experience along the way. Emma and Jake's journeys show that passion and perseverance are the true ingredients for success. So whether you're nurturing a single pot on your windowsill or cultivating a full balcony oasis, embrace the process with enthusiasm.

As you embark on your own gardening adventure, keep in mind that the possibilities are endless. Let Emma and Jake's stories inspire you to try new things and push boundaries. Set your goals high, but take small steps towards them. Celebrate your achievements and learn from your mistakes. Your container garden is not just about growing plants; it's about cultivating joy, creativity, and resilience in your life.

Consider joining local gardening groups or online communities for support and inspiration. Sharing experiences with others can provide valuable insights and encouragement. Swap tips, trade seeds, or simply enjoy the camaraderie of fellow gardeners cheering each other on.

Remember that gardening is an ongoing journey of discovery and growth—a lifelong pursuit where the rewards extend far beyond the harvest itself. Each season brings new opportunities to learn, adapt, and thrive alongside your plants. So grab your trowel, roll up your sleeves, and get ready to create something beautiful— one container at a time.

LEARNING FROM FAILURES: TURNING SETBACKS INTO GROWTH OPPORTUNITIES

Gardening, much like life, is a series of experiments. You plant seeds, nurture them, and sometimes, despite your best efforts, things don't go as planned. It's crucial to remember that setbacks are a natural part of the gardening journey. Plants may fall prey to pests or diseases, regardless of your vigilance. Maybe you chose a plant that just wasn't suited for your climate, and it struggled to survive. These moments can be disheartening, yet they are also rich with lessons waiting to be unearthed.

Reflecting on these experiences is key to growing as a gardener. Keeping a journal is an invaluable tool for this process. Document what you plant, when you plant it, and how it fares over time. Note any issues that arise and how you attempt to resolve them. This practice not only helps track progress but also creates a personal reference guide for future gardening endeavors. Reflecting on what worked and what didn't allows you to make informed decisions moving forward.

When faced with setbacks, resilience is your greatest ally. Instead of seeing failures as roadblocks, view them as opportunities for innovation. Perhaps your tomatoes didn't thrive in the pots you chose; this is a chance to research alternative varieties better suited for containers or your specific climate. Adjusting care routines based on past experiences is crucial. If a particular watering schedule didn't work before, tweak it until you find the sweet spot that keeps your plants happy and healthy.

Stories of resilience abound in the gardening community. Consider Maria, who faced a season of nutrient deficiencies that left her plants looking lackluster. She could have thrown in the towel, but chose instead to revamp her soil management practices. By incorporating organic compost and performing regular soil tests, she transformed her garden into a lush oasis by the next season. Another gardener, Paul, saw his first attempt at growing cucumbers end in failure due to early frost damage. Rather than give up, he studied methods for extending the growing season and successfully replanted, resulting in a bountiful harvest the following year.

Every setback carries the seed of a lesson. When pests invade, it might be time to explore natural pest control methods or companion planting strategies that deter those unwanted guests. If a plant isn't thriving, investigate its specific needs—perhaps it craves more sun or prefers a different soil pH. These explorations deepen your understanding and make you a more adept gardener over time.

The beauty of gardening lies in its endless cycle of growth and renewal. Each season presents new challenges and triumphs, teaching patience and perseverance along the way. Embrace this ongoing learning process with an open heart and a curious mind. You'll find that with each mistake comes the opportunity for creativity and discovery—a chance to reinvent your garden with newfound wisdom.

Setbacks shouldn't deter your enthusiasm for gardening; rather, they should fuel your determination to improve. As you gain experience, you'll learn to anticipate potential issues before they become significant problems. Your confidence will grow alongside your plants, leading to increasingly successful seasons.

Remember that every gardener has faced failures. It's part of what makes gardening such a rewarding pursuit—overcoming challenges and witnessing your hard work come to fruition. Whether it's battling pesky aphids or coaxing reluctant seeds to sprout, each step of the process contributes to your growth as a gardener.

Your garden is a reflection of your resilience and adaptability. Celebrate each small victory—a sprouting seedling or a blooming flower—as proof of your dedication and passion. Let these moments inspire you to continue nurturing your space with love and determination.

Your journey through gardening's ups and downs will shape you into a resourceful and knowledgeable gardener capable of tackling any challenge thrown your way. Embrace the failures as part of the process; they are stepping stones on the path to success in the world of container gardening.

COMMUNITY CONNECTIONS: JOINING THE CONTAINER GARDENING MOVEMENT

Imagine the joy of walking into a room filled with people who share your passion for growing things, eagerly swapping stories about their latest gardening triumphs and challenges. Joining a community of fellow container gardeners can be a game-changer. It opens the door to a wealth of shared knowledge and resources that can transform your gardening experience. When you connect with others, you tap into a collective brain trust, gaining access to tips and techniques that might take years to learn on your own. This network is invaluable, offering advice and support when you're stumped by a stubborn plant problem or need a fresh idea for your next project.

Building friendships within a gardening community doesn't just enrich your gardening life; it also enriches your personal life. These connections often extend beyond the garden, creating lasting relationships and support networks. Whether you're swapping seeds or organizing a group trip to the local nursery, the camaraderie of a gardening community is something special. You'll find yourself not only growing plants but also growing friendships that are rooted in shared experiences and a mutual love for the earth.

Finding these communities is easier than you might think. Local gardening clubs or meetups are fantastic places to start. These groups often host regular meetings where you can learn from more experienced gardeners and share your own insights. If in-person meetings aren't your style, online forums and social media groups offer an alternative. Platforms like Facebook and Reddit have thriving gardening communities where you can ask questions, share photos of your progress, and get advice from people all around the world.

The beauty of these communities lies in their collaborative spirit. Organizing plant swaps or seed exchanges is a popular activity that not only diversifies your garden but also fosters a sense of community. Imagine trading a few of your thriving basil seedlings for a neighbor's heirloom tomato plants—both of you walk away enriched by the exchange. Community garden projects take this collaboration to another level, allowing you to work alongside others to create something beautiful that benefits everyone involved.

The impact of community involvement on personal growth cannot be overstated. When you're surrounded by supportive peers, learning new techniques becomes a shared adventure rather than a solitary task. Seasoned gardeners often take newcomers under their wing, offering guidance that boosts confidence and accelerates learning. Seeing what others have achieved in their own gardens is incredibly motivating; it spurs you on to try new things and push your own boundaries.

Witnessing community achievements firsthand can ignite a passion for experimentation and innovation in your own garden. You might find yourself inspired to try growing an unusual vegetable variety simply because someone in your group has done so successfully. Or perhaps you'll adopt a new method for improving soil health after hearing about the positive results it brought to another gardener's plot.

Participating in these communities also provides an opportunity to give back by sharing your own knowledge and experiences. As you grow in confidence and skill, you'll find yourself offering tips to newcomers who are just starting out. This exchange of ideas and experiences strengthens the community as a whole, creating an environment where everyone learns and grows together.

The role of community in personal growth extends beyond just acquiring new skills; it fosters a sense of belonging and purpose. When you're part of something larger than yourself, your successes feel even more rewarding because they're shared with others who understand the journey. The encouragement and recognition from fellow gardeners boost morale and inspire further exploration.

As you become more involved in gardening communities, you'll likely discover areas where you can contribute uniquely. Perhaps you have a knack for organizing events or an eye for design that helps others plan their garden layouts. Sharing these talents enhances the community while allowing you to develop skills that go beyond gardening.

In essence, joining the container gardening movement is about more than cultivating plants; it's about cultivating connections, creativity, and community spirit. Whether you're attending your first meetup or logging into an online forum for tips on pest control, remember that every interaction is an opportunity to grow —not just as a gardener but as part of a vibrant, supportive network dedicated to making the world a greener place.

PLANNING FOR THE FUTURE: EXPANDING YOUR GARDENING HORIZONS

Picture yourself standing on your balcony or patio, immersing yourself in the lush beauty of your thriving container garden. It's amazing how such a small space, full of potential, can transform into a spectacular oasis of greenery and vitality. Envision a future where your garden becomes not only a source of aesthetic pleasure and daily relaxation but also a bountiful supplier of fresh, home-grown produce. Planning and setting realistic goals for your garden can be both invigorating and motivating. As you ponder your gardening ambitions, consider what you wish to achieve. Could it be an expanded herb collection to elevate your culinary creations, an enhanced assortment of vegetables to yield a plentiful harvest throughout the seasons, or an integration of flowering plants that provide a painterly splash of color year-round? Whatever your unique vision may encompass, formulating clear and achievable goals will effectively chart the course for your gardening journey ahead.

Expanding your garden need not be a rapid endeavor; in fact, gradual and measured growth often yields the most satisfying and sustainable results. Start by methodically adding new containers to your space. This incremental approach allows you to carefully manage the additional responsibilities, ensuring that each new plant receives the individualized attention and care it deserves. By introducing new varieties slowly, you grant yourself the necessary time to thoroughly acquaint yourself with the specific demands and attributes of each plant. This considered approach makes calibrating your care routines more intuitive and seamless. Slowly broadening your garden's diversity will create a vibrant, interconnected tapestry of plants that thrive symbiotically, enhancing both productivity and aesthetic value.

For those poised to delve into more sophisticated techniques, the world of gardening is replete with splendid opportunities and novel methodologies. Imagine venturing into the realms of hydroponics or aquaponics—innovative systems that allow plant cultivation without the traditional reliance on soil, instead utilizing nutrient-rich water. These cutting-edge techniques are especially appealing for those facing spatial limitations, as they optimize profitability and yield. Incorporating smart technology within your garden can revolutionize your approach to nurturing plants. Consider employing sensors or apps that meticulously monitor crucial elements like soil moisture, ambient temperature, and light exposure. The integration of technology can significantly optimize plant health, rendering garden management more streamlined and effective.

As you continue to cultivate and enrich your container garden, adopt a mindset of lifelong learning and adaptability. The field of gardening is one of constant evolution, with exciting trends and innovations emerging at a steady pace. Immerse yourself in advanced gardening literature or consider enrolling in specialized courses to deepen your understanding and inspire novel ideas. Staying informed about groundbreaking practices not only benefits your garden but also maintains your enthusiasm and fulfillment as a gardener. Adaptability is essential to flourishing within the gardening community; embracing change and innovation infuses your garden with vitality and resilience.

Planning for the future of your garden transcends mere physical expansion; it's fundamentally about nurturing a mindset of growth, exploration, and curiosity. As you articulate your goals and experiment with new methodologies, remember that gardening is a voyage of discovery, teeming with opportunities to learn and develop in harmony with your plants. Whether you're dreaming of harvesting vine-ripened tomatoes or crafting a sanctuary that invites the comforting buzz of pollinators, each deliberate step taken brings you closer to realizing your gardening dreams.

In conclusion, envisioning the future of your container garden involves dreaming boldly while undertaking small, deliberate steps toward realizing those dreams. Your garden is not just a collection of plants; it's a living canvas for creativity, a space that invites you to experiment with ideas and embrace the potential of what a seemingly modest space can offer. Through mindful planning and a harmonious blend of technology and tradition, you can cultivate a garden that genuinely resonates with your personal style and values, meeting both your practical needs and aesthetic desires.

KEEP THE GARDEN GROWING

Now that you've learned how to grow your own veggies, herbs, and flowers in containers, you've got everything you need to turn even the smallest space into a garden.

But here's something else you can grow—**a little encouragement** for the next person just getting started.

By sharing your honest thoughts about this book on Amazon, you'll help others find the same tips and confidence that helped you. It's like leaving a trail of sunshine for the next gardener to follow.

Thank you for being part of this growing community. Container gardening keeps blooming when we share what we've learned—and you're helping make that happen.

☞ **Scan the QR code or go here to leave your review on Amazon:** https://www.amazon.com/review/review-your-purchas es/?asin=B0F8KB1V1L

Thanks again—and happy planting!

– Avery Sage

CONCLUSION

As we wrap up this journey together, let's take a moment to appreciate how far you've come. Just a while ago, the idea of creating your own container garden might have seemed daunting. But look at you now, armed with knowledge and confidence, ready to transform any small space into a lush, vibrant oasis.

This book has walked you through the essentials of container gardening. We started with understanding the basics, like choosing the right containers and creating the perfect soil mix. We explored the art of selecting and caring for plants, whether they are vegetables, herbs, or flowers. We delved into watering techniques, fertilization strategies, and even how to deal with pests and diseases naturally. Each chapter was designed to build your skills step-by-step, making the process approachable and enjoyable.

Key takeaways from our journey include the importance of understanding your plants' needs. From sunlight and water to nutrients and space, every element plays a role in their health. You've learned how to identify and solve common problems, ensuring your plants thrive. And let's not forget the creative aspects —designing your garden layout, experimenting with vertical gardening, and integrating companion planting for a harmonious ecosystem.

Now, I invite you to take action. If you haven't started your container garden yet, now is the time. Use this book as your guide, but don't be afraid to experiment and make it your own. Try new plant combinations, explore different gardening techniques, and most importantly, have fun with it. Your garden is a reflection of your creativity and care, and there's no right or wrong way to grow it.

Looking ahead, envision your future as a gardener. Imagine your space filled with thriving plants, each one a testament to your dedication and growth. Consider how this journey might inspire you to expand your garden, try new techniques, or even share your newfound knowledge with others. The possibilities are endless, and your garden will grow with you as you continue to learn and explore.

Remember, gardening is not just a hobby; it's a lifelong journey. There will be moments of triumph and times of challenge, but each experience adds to your story. Embrace the process, celebrate the small victories, and learn from the setbacks. Your garden is your canvas, and you are the artist.

As we conclude, I want to thank you for choosing to embark on this journey with me. Your commitment to learning and growing is truly inspiring. I hope this book has equipped you with the tools and confidence to create a beautiful, flourishing container garden. May it bring you joy, peace, and a deeper connection to the natural world. Happy gardening!

REFERENCES

1. themicrogardener.com. (2025). *The Benefits of Container Gardening.* https://themicrogardener.com/the-benefits-of-container-gardening/
2. gardenerspath.com. (2025). *Containers, Pots, and Planters: What Material Is Best?* https://gardenerspath.com/how-to/containers/plant-containers-pots-planters-material-best/
3. extension.psu.edu. (2025). *Homemade Potting Media.* https://extension.psu.edu/homemade-potting-media
4. www.farmstandapp.com. (2025). *12 Container Gardening for Urban Spaces Tips That ...* https://www.farmstandapp.com/6011/container-gardening-for-urban-spaces/
5. extension.umd.edu. (2025). *Growing Vegetables in Containers.* https://extension.umd.edu/resource/growing-vegetables-containers
6. gardenary.com. (2025). *How to Grow Lots of Herbs in a Small Space - Gardenary.* https://www.gardenary.com/blog/how-to-grow-herbs-in-a-small-space
7. hgtv.com. (2025). *24 Easy Flowers for Beginners to Grow.* https://www.hgtv.com/outdoors/flowers-and-plants/flowers/13-cant-kill-flowers-for-beginners-pictures
8. permacultureapartment.com. (2025). *Container Garden Companion Planting Guide.* https://www.permacultureapartment.com/post/container-garden-companion-planting
9. rainbird.com. (2025). *How to Plan an Automatic Drip Watering System ...* https://www.rainbird.com/homeowners/blog/how-to-plan-an-automatic-drip-watering-system-for-container-plants
10. earthbox.com. (2025). *Planter Boxes: 10 Benefits for Urban Gardening.* https://earthbox.com/blog/planter-boxes-for-urban-gardening
11. milorganite.com. (2025). *Organic vs Synthetic Fertilizer - Milorganite.* https://www.milorganite.com/lawn-care/organic-lawn-care/organic-vs-synthetic
12. plushbeds.com. (2025). *13 Ways to Implement Water Conservation in Your Garden.* https://www.plushbeds.com/blogs/green-sleep/13-ways-to-implement-water-conservation-in-your-garden
13. rootsandrefuge.com. (2025). *A Complete Guide to Vertical Gardening (On a Budget!)* https://rootsandrefuge.com/vertical-gardening-on-a-budget/

14. finegardening.com. (2025). *The Elements of Great Garden-Container Design* ... https://www.finegardening.com/article/the-elements-of-great-garden-container-design-simplified

15. vickiodell.com. (2025). *15 Upcycled Container Projects*. https://vickiodell.com/15-upcycled-container-projects/

16. xerces.org. (2025). *Pollinator-Friendly Native Plant Lists*. https://xerces.org/pollinator-conservation/pollinator-friendly-plant-lists

17. gardeningknowhow.com. (2025). *Container Garden Pest Control*. https://www.gardeningknowhow.com/special/containers/container-pests.htm

18. eartheasy.com. (2025). *Natural Garden Pest Control: Safe, Non-Toxic Methods* ... https://learn.eartheasy.com/guides/natural-garden-pest-control/

19. dummies.com. (2025). *Common Plant Diseases in Container Gardens*. https://www.dummies.com/article/home-auto-hobbies/garden-green-living/gardening/containers/common-plant-diseases-in-container-gardens-180895/

20. npic.orst.edu. (2025). *Beneficial Insects - National Pesticide Information Center*. https://npic.orst.edu/envir/beneficial/index.html

21. themicrogardener.com. (2025). *Guide to Understanding Microclimates in your Garden*. https://themicrogardener.com/guide-understanding-microclimates-in-your-garden/

22. planthardiness.ars.usda.gov. (2025). *USDA Plant Hardiness Zone Map*. https://planthardiness.ars.usda.gov/

23. fbfs.com. (2025). *How to Protect Crops From Extreme Weather*. https://www.fbfs.com/learning-center/protect-crops-from-extreme-weather

24. cyclandscaping.com. (2025). *Principles Of Xeriscaping And Its Benefits*. https://cyclandscaping.com/principles-of-xeriscaping-and-its-benefits/

25. piedmontmastergardeners.org. (2025). *Home Composting Solutions For Virtually Everyone*. https://piedmontmastergardeners.org/article/composting-options-for-small-indoor-and-restricted-spaces/

26. bhg.com. (2025). *24 Unique Repurposed Planters Made from Salvaged* ... https://www.bhg.com/gardening/container/plans-ideas/beyond-the-ordinary-flowerpot/

27. ngb.org. (2025). *The Ultimate Guide to Water-Wise Gardening*. https://ngb.org/water-wise-gardening-plants/

28. esteelicious.com. (2025). *Top 5 Natural Pest Control Methods for Container Gardens*. https://www.esteelicious.com/top-5-natural-pest-control-methods-for-container-gardens/

29. provenwinners.com. (2025). *10 Container Gardening Mistakes to Avoid.* https://www.provenwinners.com/learn/top-ten-lists/10-container-gardening-mistakes-avoid

30. pubs.ext.vt.edu. (2025). *Diagnosing Plant Problems | VCE Publications - Virginia Tech.* https://www.pubs.ext.vt.edu/426/426-714/426-714.html

31. homestead.org. (2025). *Container Gardening in the City: Urban Homesteading on ...* https://www.homestead.org/gardening/container-gardening-in-the-city-urban-homesteading-on-a-budget/

32. isminc.com. (2025). *10 Reasons to Join a Community Garden.* https://isminc.com/advisory/publications/the-source/10-reasons-to-join-a-community-garden